GENESIS to REVELATION

A Comprehensive Verse-by-Verse Exploration of the Bible

JOHN
WOODROW A. GEIER

LEADER GUIDE

GENESIS to REVELATION

A Comprehensive Verse-by-Verse Exploration of the Bible

JOHN
WOODROW A. GEIER

LEADER GUIDE

GENESIS TO REVELATION SERIES: **JOHN**
LEADER GUIDE

ABINGDON PRESS
Nashville
Copyright © 1984, 1985, 1987 by Graded Press.
Revised Edition Copyright © 1997 by Abingdon Press.
Updated and Revised Edition Copyright © 2017 by Abingdon Press
All rights reserved.

ISBN 978-1-5018-4859-9

Manufactured in the United States of America
17 18 19 20 21 22 23 24 25 26—10 9 8 7 6 5 4 3 2 1

HOW TO TEACH GENESIS TO REVELATION

Unique Features of This Bible Study

In Genesis to Revelation, you and your class will study the Bible in three steps. Each step provides a different level of understanding of the Scripture. We call these steps Dimension One, Dimension Two, and Dimension Three.

Dimension One concerns what the Bible actually says. You do not interpret the Scripture at this point; you merely take account of what it says. Your main goal for this dimension is to get the content of the passage clear in your mind. What does the Bible say?

Dimension One is in workbook form. The members of the class will write the answers to questions about the passage in the space provided in the participant book. All the questions in Dimension One can be answered by reading the Bible itself. Be sure the class finishes Dimension One before going on to Dimensions Two and Three.

Dimension Two concerns information that will shed light on the Scripture under consideration. Dimension Two will answer such questions as

- What are the original meanings of some of the words used in the passage?

- What is the original background of the passage?

- Why was the passage most likely written?

- What are the relationships between the persons mentioned in the passage?

- What geographical and cultural factors affect the meaning of the passage?

The question for Dimension Two is, What information do we need in order to understand the meaning of the passage? In Dimension One the class members will discover what the Bible says. In Dimension Two they will discover what the Bible means.

Dimension Three focuses on interpreting the Scripture and applying it to life situations. The questions here are

- What is the meaning of the passage for my life?

- What response does the passage require of me as a Christian?

- What response does this passage require of us as a group?

Dimension Three questions have no easy answers. The task of applying the Scripture to life situations is up to you and the class.

Aside from the three-dimensional approach, another unique feature of this study is the organization of the series as a whole. Classes that choose to study the Genesis to Revelation Series will be able to study all the books of the Bible in their biblical order. This method will give the class continuity that is not present in most other Bible studies. The class will read and study virtually every verse of the Bible, from Genesis straight through to Revelation.

Weekly Preparation

Begin planning for each session early in the week. Read the passage that the lesson covers, and write the answers to Dimension One questions in the participant book. Then read Dimensions Two and Three in the participant book. Make a note of any questions or comments you have. Finally, study the material in the leader guide carefully. Decide how you want to organize your class session.

Organizing the Class Session

Since Genesis to Revelation involves three steps in studying the Scripture, you will want to organize your class sessions around these three dimensions. Each lesson in the participant book and this leader guide consists of three parts.

The first part of each lesson in the leader guide is the same as the Dimension One section in the participant book, except that the leader guide includes the answers to Dimension One questions. These questions and answers are taken from the New International Version of the Bible.

You might use Dimension One in several ways:

1. Ask the group members to read the Scripture and to write the answers to all the Dimension One questions before coming to class. This method will require that the class covenant to spend the necessary amount of study time outside of class. When the class session begins, read through the Dimension One questions, asking for responses from the group members. If anyone needs help with any of the answers, look at the biblical reference together.

2. Or, if you have enough class time, you might spend the first part of the session working through the Dimension One questions together as a group. Locate the Scripture references, ask the questions one at a time, and invite the class members to find the answers and to read them aloud. Then allow enough time for them to write the answers in the participant book.

3. Or, take some time at the beginning of the class session for group members to work individually. Have them read the Dimension One questions and the Scripture references and then write their answers to the questions in the spaces provided in the participant book. Discuss together any questions or answers in Dimension One that do not seem clear. This approach may take longer than the others, but it provides a good change of pace from time to time.

You do not have to organize your class sessions the same way every week. Ask the class members what they prefer. Experiment! You may find ways to study the Dimension One material other than the ones listed above.

The second part of each lesson in this leader guide corresponds to the second part of the participant book lessons. The Dimension Two section of the participant book provides background information to help the participants understand the Scripture. Become familiar with the information in the participant book.

Dimension Two of this leader guide contains additional information on the passage. The leader guide goes into more depth with some parts of the passage than the participant book does. You will want to share this information with the group in whatever way seems appropriate. For example, if someone raises a question about a particular verse, share any additional background information from the leader guide.

You might raise a simple question such as, What words or phrases gave you trouble in understanding the passage? or, Having grasped the content of the passage, what questions remain in your mind? Encourage the group members to share confusing points, troublesome words or phrases, or lingering questions. Write these problems on a posterboard or markerboard. This list of concerns will form the outline for the second portion of the session.

These concerns may also stimulate some research on the part of the group members. If your study group is large enough, divide the class into three groups. Then divide the passage for the following week into three parts. Assign a portion of the passage to each group. Using Bible commentaries and Bible dictionaries, direct each group to discover as much as it can about this portion of the passage before the class meets again. Each group will then report its findings during the class session.

The third part of each lesson in this leader guide relates to Dimension Three in the participant book. This section helps class members discover how to apply the Scripture to their own lives. Here you will find one or more interpretations of the passage—whether traditional, historical, or contemporary. Use these interpretations when appropriate to illumine the passage for the group members.

Dimension Three in the participant book points out some of the issues in the passage that are relevant to our lives. For each of these issues, the participant book raises questions to help the participants assess the meaning of the Scripture for their lives. The information in Dimension Three of the leader guide is designed to help you lead the class in discussing these issues. Usually, you will find a more in-depth discussion of portions of the Scripture.

The discussion in the leader guide will give you a better perspective on the Scripture and its interpretation before you begin to assess its meaning for today. You will probably want to share this Dimension Three information with the class to open the discussion. For each life situation, the leader guide contains suggestions on facilitating the class discussion. You, as the leader, are responsible for group discussions of Dimension Three issues.

Assembling Your Materials

You will need at least three items to prepare for and conduct each class session:

- A leader guide
- A participant book
- A Bible—you may use any translation or several; the answers in this leader guide are taken from the New International Version.

One advantage of the Genesis to Revelation Series is that the study is self-contained. That is, all you need to lead this Bible study is provided for you in the participant books and leader guides. Occasionally, or perhaps on a regular basis, you might want to consult other sources for additional information.

HOW TO LEAD A DISCUSSION

The Teacher as Discussion Leader

As the leader of this series or a part of this series, one of your main responsibilities during each class period will be to lead the class discussion. Some leaders are apprehensive about leading a discussion. In many ways, it is easier to lecture to the class. But remember that the class members will surely benefit more from the class sessions when they actively participate in a discussion of the material.

Leading a discussion is a skill that any teacher can master with practice. And keep in mind—especially if your class is not used to discussion—that the members of your group will also be learning through practice. The following are some pointers on how to lead interesting and thought-provoking discussions in the study group.

Preparing for a Discussion—Where Do I Start?

1. Focus on the subject that will be discussed and on the goal you want to achieve through that discussion.

2. Prepare by collecting information and data that you will need; jot down these ideas, facts, and questions so that you will have them when you need them.

3. Begin organizing your ideas; stop often to review your work. Keep in mind the climate within the group—attitudes, feelings, eagerness to participate and learn.

4. Consider possible alternative group procedures. Be prepared for the unexpected.

5. Having reached your goal, think through several ways to bring the discussion to a close.

As the leader, do not feel that your responsibility is to give a full account or report of the assigned material. This practice promotes dependency. Instead, through stimulating questions and discussion, the participants will read the material—not because you tell them to but because they want to read and prepare.

How Do I Establish a Climate for Learning?

The leader's readiness and preparation quickly establish a climate in which the group can proceed and its members learn and grow. The anxiety and fear of an unprepared leader are contagious but so are the positive vibrations coming from a leader who is prepared to move into a learning enterprise.

An attitude of shared ownership is also basic. Group members need to perceive themselves as part of the learning experience. Persons establish ownership by working on goals, sharing concerns, and accepting major responsibility for learning.

Here are several ways the leader can foster a positive climate for learning and growth.

1. Readiness. A leader who is always fully prepared can promote, in turn, the group's readiness to learn.

2. Exploration. When the leader encourages group members to freely explore new ideas, persons will know they are in a group whose primary function is learning.

3. Exposure. A leader who is open, honest, and willing to reveal himself or herself to the group will encourage participants to discuss their feelings and opinions.

4. Confidentiality. A leader can create a climate for learning when he or she respects the confidentiality of group members and encourages the group members to respect one another's confidentiality.

5. Acceptance. When a leader shows a high degree of acceptance, participants can likewise accept one another honestly.

How Can I Deal With Conflict?

What if conflict or strong disagreement arises in your group? What do you do? Think about the effective and ineffective ways you have dealt with conflict in the past.

Group conflict may come from one of several sources. One common source of conflict involves personality clashes. Any group is almost certain to contain at least two persons whose personalities clash. If you break your class into smaller groups for discussion, be sure these persons are in separate groups.

Another common source of group conflict is subject matter. The Bible can be a very controversial subject. Remember the difference between discussion or disagreement and conflict. As a leader you will have to decide when to encourage discussion and when to discourage conflict that is destructive to the group process.

Group conflict may also come from a general atmosphere conducive to expression of ideas and opinions. Try to discourage persons in the group from being judgmental toward others and their ideas. Keep reminding the class that each person is entitled to his or her own opinions and that no one opinion is more valid than another.

How Much Should I Contribute to the Discussion?

Many leaders are unsure about how much they should contribute to the class discussions. Below are several pitfalls to avoid.

1. The leader should remain neutral on a question until the group has had adequate time to discuss it. At the proper time in the discussion the leader can offer his or her opinion. The leader can direct the questions to the group at large, rechanneling those questions that come to him or her.

    At times when the members need to grapple with a question or issue, the most untimely response a leader can make is answering the question. Do not fall into the trap of doing the group members' work for them. Let them struggle with the question.

    However, if the leader has asked the group members to reveal thoughts and feelings, then group members have the right to expect the same of the leader. A leader has no right to ask others to reveal something he or she is unwilling to reveal. A leader can reveal thoughts and feelings, but at the appropriate time.

    The refusal to respond immediately to a question often takes self-discipline. The leader has spent time thinking, reading, and preparing. Thus the leader usually does have a point of view, and waiting for others to respond calls for restraint.

2. Another pitfall is the leader's making a speech or extended comments in expressing an opinion or summarizing what has been said. For example, in an attempt to persuade others, a leader may speak, repeat, or strongly emphasize what someone says concerning a question.

3. Finally, the pitfall of believing the leader must know "the answers" to the questions is always apparent. The leader need not know all the answers. Many questions that should be raised are ultimate and unanswerable; other questions are open-ended; and still others have several answers.

GENESIS TO REVELATION SERIES
JOHN Leader Guide

Table of Contents

About the Writer
Dr. Woodrow A. Geier served as a pastor and as an editor of adult curriculum resources for The United Methodist Church.

Out of his fullness we have all received grace in place of grace already given (1:16).

1

THE GOOD NEWS— FULLNESS OF HIS GRACE

John 1:1-2:11

DIMENSION ONE: WHAT DOES THE BIBLE SAY?

Answer these questions by reading John 1

1. What words of Genesis do the first three words of John's Gospel recall? (1:1; Genesis 1:1)
   John's Gospel and the Book of Genesis both open with the words "In the beginning."

2. What words of John suggest Jesus' divine nature? (1:2-4)
   John says that "In the beginning was the Word [Jesus], and the Word was with God"; that he was part of the creation of all things; and that "in him was life, and that life was the light of all mankind."

3. What does John tell us about the relationship between life and light, light and darkness? (1:4-5)
   John tells us that light gives life and overcomes darkness.

4. Who is introduced into the Prologue of the Gospel in 1:6?
   "A man sent from God," named John, is introduced in verse 6.

5. What is John's purpose? (1:7-8)

John's purpose is "to testify concerning that light, so that through him all might believe." John is not that light.

6. To whom did the true light come? (1:11)

"He came to that which was his own" and was not received.

7. What was given to those who believed and did receive him? (1:12-13)

Those who believed received the right to became children of God.

8. What did the people ("we all") receive in the coming of the Son? (1:16-17)

"We have all received grace in place of grace already given. . . . grace and truth came through Jesus Christ."

9. How does John's Gospel describe John the Baptist? (1:23)

John says of himself, "I am the voice of one calling in the wilderness."

10. Where is John baptizing? (1:28)

John is baptizing "at Bethany on the other side of the Jordan."

11. How does John say that he recognized Jesus? (1:32)

John says that he "saw the Spirit come down from heaven as a dove and remain on him."

12. Who are Jesus' first disciples, as listed by our writer? (1:40-51)

Jesus' first disciples named in John are Andrew, Simon Peter, Philip, and Nathanael.

Answer these questions by reading John 2:1-11

13. Who attended the marriage feast at Cana of Galilee? (2:1-2)

Jesus, his mother, and his disciples attended the marriage feast.

14. What did Jesus say to the servants? (2:7-8)

    Jesus told the servants to "fill the jars with water" and to take some of the water to the master of the banquet.

15. What did the master of the banquet say about the wine? (2:10)

    The master seemed surprised the good wine had been saved and served last.

16. What did Jesus achieve by the first of his "signs"? (2:11)

    Jesus "revealed his glory, and his disciples believed in him."

DIMENSION TWO: WHAT DOES THE BIBLE MEAN?

Introduction. Most of us have been confronted by John's Gospel. In Sunday school we have heard stories from it. In worship services we have heard sermons based on it and have participated in the liturgy drawn from the Gospel. The words of John have comforted us at funerals and given courage in times of uncertainty, anxiety, disappointment, and stress. So John's Gospel is already a part of us, already a present help.

We shall approach the Gospel as a personal message of God—through the unknown author John—to the church and to us. We want to concentrate on bringing out the permanent values of John for us today.

Many studies of John begin by speculating on who wrote the book, whether it was from the hand of one author, when and where the book was written, the Hellenistic (Greek) and Jewish influences in the Gospel, and the relationship of John to the other Gospels. These are important questions, but they are not central to the present study. We do not want to approach the Gospel as a mysterious puzzle to be solved. We want to see it as a portrait of Jesus Christ and an account of what God is doing through him.

So when we read John's Gospel, we should be primarily concerned with what arises in our minds and hearts as we read, with what the Holy Spirit says to us through the printed page. The Word of God is not printed propositions. It is a living, personal Word that reaches us in the depths of our being.

The Word is Jesus Christ, God's personal self-communication to us. In this study, therefore, we should think of John's Gospel as a personal letter of God, telling us about Jesus Christ and his mission of love to us and to the whole earth. John's Gospel is God's Word already spoken to our desolation. It is the proclamation that in Christ the eternal God has triumphed over sin and death.

The study should help us get a sharp focus on the whole of the Gospel of John. You know what happens when a photographer simply and carelessly lifts a camera, randomly presses a button, and then develops the film. Because the photographer failed to study the whole setting and its light and shadows, the camera failed to get a picture that was worth the effort. Such picture-taking may warn us of errors we may commit in the study of the Fourth Gospel.

To get to the heart of any literary composition we have to understand the author's purpose. The author of John makes his purpose clear: "Jesus performed many other signs in the presence of his disciples, which are not recorded in this book. But these are written that you may believe that Jesus is the Messiah, the Son of God, and that by believing you may have life in his name" (20:30-31).

John 1:1-18. We turn to the Prologue. If a class member is familiar with musical productions, ask that person to discuss the functions of the overture and its place in an opera or a symphony. Point out that an overture presents and repeats the musical themes from the rest of the production. An overture acts as a teaser, making the listener eager to hear more of the theme music as it is presented throughout the symphony or opera. Why is this term appropriate for the discussion of the Prologue to the Gospel of John?

John 1:1-18 is also like the lead paragraph of a journalistic article. It serves to hold the whole composition together. It suggests to the reader the direction the author is going. It defines the area of discussion.

Read John 1:1-18 aloud. This section of John is poetry except for verses 6-8 and 15. Why would the author choose a poem to introduce the Gospel?

Poetry is a special way for writer and reader to share in truth. Poets deal in images and rhythms that evoke deep responses from readers. The poet sees. He or she cuts away humdrum language and conveys to us a sense of meaning and value in writing that otherwise might be meaningless. Poets stimulate deeper appreciations and perceptions of the reader. They do this through the beauty of their words. This beauty consists in fresh images, rhythm, and meter.

The poet's words create a power that is controlled and concentrated by the rhythm. The poet's words constitute a formula for us so that our minds are freed from dullness and distraction. The formula possesses power. The words become a part of us when they have been merged into a formula. A formula musters power because each word affects us strongly. Words that are metrically organized—such as you have just read in John's Gospel—develop an abiding hold on us. Consider these lines:

> Do not let your hearts be troubled
> and do not be afraid.
>
> —John 14:27c

The rhythm of words is enhanced by firm control—as in the Psalms—through repetition, parallelism, refrain, or alliterative verse (using the same initial sound for words in the same line or at the beginning of each line). In our English poetry the rhythm is largely enhanced through rhyme.

True poetry is therefore the most imaginative, most forceful, and most effective way of saying something. We long remember such lines as we have quoted from the Prologue because they are the bearers of all the qualities of poetry.

Beautiful words are always the most powerful and creative words. So poetry provides the order, power, and simplification that enable us to understand a subject. Note the order, power, and simplification of the words of the Prologue.

The poetry of the Prologue is taken from Greek and Hebrew sources, but scholars think it is more a product of the latter. John has appropriated the Hebrew idea of cosmic wisdom that is beautifully described in Proverbs 8 and 9, especially in Proverbs 8. Read these two chapters in Proverbs to identify points at which John has taken the ideas of divine wisdom.

The chapters in Proverbs present the Hebrew concept of the preexistent divine Wisdom that has created the world. John's understanding of this reality parallels that of the apostle Paul: "Christ the power of God and the wisdom of God" (1 Corinthians 1:24). John and Paul want to affirm the continuity of the Old Testament revelation with that of the new revelations in Jesus, who will be revealed as the Christ.

The Word in John's Prologue speaks to our universal and persisting human need for an ordered, coordinating principle that will hold the world together for us. We cannot live without some sense of relationship between things. We all need to make sense of existence. We do not like a disordered household or a world where machines run amuck. Our human nature seems to demand a principle and a power that governs all life. The doctrine of the Word speaks to this deep need of ours for order and dependability.

Discuss our human need for order and dependability. Give some examples of the lack of order and dependability. Ask class members for their reactions to a disorderly existence. Do they think the author of John is challenging readers to attain orderly minds? How?

Read and discuss Genesis 1:31. How does John reaffirm this verse? Why do you think the Prologue begins with the words, *In the beginning*?

Discuss the material in the participant book on page 10 that begins "John also introduces . . ."). Why were Jesus' own people rejecting him?

Discuss John's words contrasting light and darkness. Why do you think John concentrates on the conflict between the two? Light brings life, enlightenment, knowledge, and healing. What else does light represent?

Summarize the material on rebirth in the middle of page 11 in the participant book. What do you think *rebirth* means? (Make a note of class members' responses, and hold the notes for discussion of John 3:16 in the next lesson.)

The doctrine of the Word answers the deepest questions of the human heart. Who is this Jesus and what does he have to say to me? You know how it is to hear a knock on your door at midnight when the world is hushed and sleeping. Your first question of the intruder or friend is, "Who are you?" Everything then depends on the answer you get. Unless we know who Jesus is, we cannot know what he has to say to us. But when we know who Jesus is and receive him in faith (personal trust and obedience), we perceive that God is saying something special to us in Jesus. Our whole existence may be altered.

The doctrine of the Word tells us that Jesus Christ is both human and divine, "true God and true man," as the Christian creeds have reminded us over the centuries. This doctrine teaches us that the most important issue of our existence is wrapped up in God's coming to us as the Word—the Word made flesh. It is the good news of the Gospel—"one blessing after another."

Our God is not an impassive, unreachable deity who sits upon a throne afar off. God comes to us. So John's Gospel bears witness to the God whose steadfast love remains forever, the God who demonstrates love in the lowly form of our human existence. We have all received of God's fullness—"full of grace and truth."

Now the living Word has come. "For the law was given through Moses; grace and truth came through Jesus Christ" (1:17). Jesus reveals the God who is unseen. He does this, not only by teaching, but by his whole life poured out in love for the human race.

"We have seen his glory, the glory of the one and only Son, who came from the Father" (1:14b). The Jewish people held to a deep conviction that no one could see God's face directly and live. Exodus 33:18-23 gives us the classic treatment of this theme in the Old Testament. Here Moses says, "Now show me your glory." God replies that the divine face Moses cannot see, but that the divine glory will be present: "I will cause all my goodness to pass in front of you, and I will proclaim my name, the LORD, in your presence. I will have mercy on whom I will have mercy, and I will have compassion on whom I will have compassion."

The story of the Old Testament and the New Testament is the passing of God's redemptive mercy before us. God's glory is God's love in action, God's mighty deeds for our deliverance from sin. John 1:14-17 tells us that God's glory resided in the flesh (the human nature) of Jesus Christ. God's grace (God's love that redeems from evil) and God's truth (faithfulness to God's promises) are incarnate in Jesus Christ, who took on himself our human nature. These qualities are available to all people. They are the inexhaustible gift of God's fullness of grace that fulfills the law of Moses.

All this leads us to the conclusion that the main truth of the Christian faith is that the eternal Son of God has taken our humanity on himself. He bridges the gulf between the human and the divine. He is the mediator between God and us, the divine-human Redeemer. In Jesus Christ, God makes God's self known; God unites the human and the divine. In Jesus Christ, God meets us where we are; and God's revelation is God's search for us where we are. God does not simply wait for us to seek God. God seeks us.

Recall the story of Moses' encounter with the glory of God (Exodus 3:1-6). What does this story have to do with the words "we have seen his glory" (John 1:14)? How do you think Christ is the mediator between God and God's human children?

Close your discussion of John 1:1-18 with an examination of the meaning of *grace*.

John 1:19-34. In John's Gospel we are reminded quite forcefully that John the Baptist is not the light and that Jesus is far above John even before Jesus' name is mentioned. Nothing of John's ministry is reported, only his testimony concerning Jesus. When John sees Jesus approaching, he recognizes him immediately and says, "Look, the Lamb of God, who takes away the sin of the world! . . . I have seen and I testify that this is God's Chosen One" (1:29, 34). How does the Baptist figure in the mission of Jesus?

John 1:35-51. The account of Jesus calling his first disciples is different from the other Gospels' account of this event. (See Matthew 4:18-22; Mark 1:16-20; Luke 5:1-11.) Since these accounts cannot be reconciled, perhaps we can learn from them that the New Testament does not describe any specific way that a person has to react in order to become Jesus' follower. In John's Gospel some of Jesus' disciples come from being followers of John the Baptist. Some are introduced to Jesus by family or friends. Still others probably answered Jesus' direct call to them. What are some ways class members became Christian? How do persons today come to faith?

The writer of John ends Chapter 1 with these words of Jesus: "Very truly I tell you, you will see heaven open, and the angels of God ascending and descending on the Son of Man." Here the writer refers to the beautiful story of Jacob and the angels (Genesis 28:10-17). He also uses the term *Son of Man* to apply to Jesus' mission. Why does Jesus use the term *Son of Man* to apply to himself? This title is used often in John's Gospel. Here it means the disclosure of God's attributes in human form—the work of the Messiah.

Son of Man also represents the authority of Jesus to introduce into the present the judgment pronounced on all who accept or reject him who is in the world on God's mission.

John 2:1-11. The account of the wedding at Cana is a complete story in itself. The beginning of the account is "On the third day," which may be the writer's way of relating the account to the events just described—"On the third day" after calling Philip and Nathanael, which happened on "the next day" after Andrew and Peter were called (1:43). Or the writer may mean the third day of the wedding feast.

The story closes with a recognition that this work was "the first of the signs through which he [Jesus] revealed his glory" and that because of this manifestation of his glory, "his disciples believed in him" (2:11).

Read the story of the wedding feast aloud, and ask for class members' reaction to it. Why do Jesus' words to his mother seem harsh? What is Jesus' purpose?

DIMENSION THREE:
WHAT DOES THE BIBLE MEAN TO ME?

The class members may discuss the following topics or use the material in the participant book.

We Apply the Gospel to Ourselves

This closing section of the lesson should help group members find the meaning of the Scripture for their life. Make the atmosphere for your discussion informal; and encourage participants to question you, themselves, and one another.

How have class members been confronted by the Gospel of John? Ask them to quote some of their favorite verses from John. What do they think God is saying to them in these verses? How did verses from John help in times of stress and loss? What verses do we hear at funerals? What parts of John's Gospel do they use for their private devotions?

What does the Prologue mean to you? Point out the need we all have to find meaning and value for our life. How have class members found meaning and value in the passages in this lesson? Explore with them the purpose of the Prologue. What does this poem mean to them personally? Is it possible for men and women today to live creatively and constructively if they do not believe Genesis 1:31? What does the Prologue say to participants about the nature of God? about the nature of the creation? about God's purposes for their life?

Explore with class members what it means to them to believe that Jesus is both human and divine. Recall the discussion of Jesus as the mediator. How have they found Christ to be the mediator in their life?

Explore what it means to "put their faith" in Jesus Christ. Lead group members to see that Jesus insists we go beyond mere acceptance of intellectual propositions about him. To believe faithfully means we commit ourselves to Jesus Christ and what he wants in the world. Belief in Christ means having the whole weight of our love rightly directed.

God's Salvation Is at Hand

This lesson reminds us that the deepest-seated yearning of us all is for God. It centers on God in all God's infinite majesty and on the divine method of dealing with us in Jesus Christ.

This lesson goes to the heart of our search for meaning and value in life, for it challenges us to confront life's ultimate issues. It drives us to the center of the Christian revelation: the Word became flesh in Jesus Christ.

This lesson affirms the goodness of the creation and our involvement in it. A conflict between light and darkness, between good and evil exists in our world. In that conflict Christ has won the victory, and we may participate in his triumph. This lesson affirms that grace and truth have come to us in a person. The acceptance of this reality gives us confidence that God has not left us abandoned and alone on this earth.

Close by reading this quotation from *The Quest of the Historical Jesus,* by Albert Schweitzer:

> He comes to us as One unknown, without a name, as of old, by the lake-side, He came to those men who knew Him not. He speaks to us the same word: "Follow thou me!" and sets us to the tasks which He has to fulfill for our time. He commands. And to those who obey Him, whether they be wise or simple, He will reveal Himself in the toils, the conflicts, the sufferings which they shall pass through in His fellowship, and, as an ineffable mystery, they shall learn in their own experience Who He is.[1]

[1] From *The Quest of the Historical Jesus,* by Albert Schweitzer (A&C Black, Ltd., 1922), page 401.

For God so loved the world that he gave his one and only Son, that whoever believes in him shall not perish but have eternal life (3:16).

2

JESUS THE SAVIOR OF THE WORLD

John 2:12–4:54

DIMENSION ONE: WHAT DOES THE BIBLE SAY?

Answer these questions by reading John 2:12-25

1. During what great religious festival does Jesus go up to Jerusalem? (2:13)

Jesus goes up to Jerusalem for the Passover.

2. Who was in the temple, and what were they doing? (2:14)

People were selling cattle, sheep, and pigeons; others were sitting at tables exchanging money.

3. What does Jesus do and say in the temple? (2:15-16)

He makes a whip of cords and drives out the traders with their sheep and cattle. He says to "those who sold doves . . . , 'Get these out of here! Stop turning my Father's house into a market!' "

4. What is the response of the Jews, and what is Jesus' answer to them? (2:18-20)

They ask for a sign; but Jesus replies, "Destroy this temple, and I will raise it again in three days." The Jews reply that it had taken forty-six years to build the temple, "and you are going to raise it in three days?"

5. What did the disciples finally conclude about the conversation between Jesus and the Jews? (2:21-22)

After Jesus was raised from death, the disciples recalled what Jesus had said and "they believed the scripture" and him.

6. Why does Jesus not trust himself to persons who believe in him because they see the signs that he does? (2:23-25)

Jesus knows the human heart and mind ("all people"). He does not need to have anyone tell him what is in human nature.

Answer these questions by reading John 3

7. What does Nicodemus say first to Jesus? (3:1-2)

He compliments Jesus as a teacher who has come from God and says no one can perform Jesus' signs unless God is with him.

8. What does Nicodemus find hard to believe about Jesus' answer? (3:3-4)

Nicodemus does not understand Jesus' words that one must be "born again."

9. What is the heart of Jesus' message to Nicodemus? (3:16-21)

God loved the world so much that God sent his one and only Son into the world, not to condemn the world, but that those who believe in him might be saved.

10. What is John the Baptist's testimony? (3:25-30)

John testifies that the ministry of Jesus is the work of God ("what is given [him] from heaven"). John is the forerunner of the Christ, and John rejoices greatly in the ministry of Jesus.

Answer these questions by reading John 4

11. Who does Jesus meet at Jacob's well? (4:7)

Jesus meets a Samaritan woman at Jacob's well.

12. What does the Samaritan woman say when Jesus asks her for a drink? (4:9)

"You are a Jew and I am a Samaritan woman. How can you ask me for a drink?" (Jews had nothing to do with Samaritans.)

13. What does Jesus tell the woman about the water of life? (4:13-14)

The water of life that Jesus gives will quench one's thirst, because it will become "a spring of water welling up to eternal life."

14. What does Jesus say about true worship? (4:21-24)
    Jesus answers that the time is coming "when the true worshipers will worship the Father in the Spirit and in truth."

15. What is said about the Messiah in the conversation? (4:25-26)
    The Samaritan woman says that when the Messiah comes, he will explain all things. Jesus replies that he is the Messiah.

16. What is the reaction of the disciples to Jesus' conversation with the woman? (4:27)
    They are surprised to find him talking with a woman, but no one asks Jesus what he wanted or why he was talking to her.

17. Who believe in Jesus after the Samaritan woman's testimony? (4:39)
    Many Samaritans believe in Jesus.

18. What is Jesus' second sign? (4:46-54)
    Jesus heals a royal official's son.

DIMENSION TWO:
WHAT DOES THE BIBLE MEAN?

If we are to grasp readily the meaning of the stories related in this lesson's Scripture passages, we should get the events described fresh in our minds. Review these events quickly. They may be grouped into these categories:

1. Jesus' cleansing of the temple
2. Jesus' conversation with Nicodemus
3. John the Baptist's testimony about Jesus
4. Jesus' visit among the Samaritans
5. Jesus' talk with the woman at Jacob's well
6. Jesus' healing of the official's son

John 2:12-25. The problem with temple worship lay in the use of religion for profit by some people. Outward observances and conformities to ancient rituals and practices were stressed, as though reverence for the forms could bring healing and reconciliation with God. As in the time of Amos, Hosea, and other Old Testament prophets, religion was used in this way. Jesus was following in the prophetic tradition when he denounced the buying and selling of animal sacrifices as a means of gaining God's favor. God is pleased by worship that springs from the heart and from pure motives. God delights in the worship of persons who seek to do the divine will—persons who are concerned with right relationships with God and with their neighbors. The prophets insisted that justice should "roll on like a river . . . like a never-failing stream" (Amos 5:24), that oppression of the poor must cease, and that peace be diligently sought. Jesus was severe in his condemnation of self-centered religion that would make the "Father's house into a market."

In driving the traders from the temple, Jesus dealt with a problem that has persisted in every society, every religion, every Christian denomination. That problem is the exploitation of religious feelings and loyalties for worldly gain. The mixed-up religious and secular leaders of the Middle Ages did this when they launched crusades to wrest the tomb of Jesus from the "infidels." The buyers and sellers of indulgences in the day of Martin Luther did this when they presumed to forgive sins following payment of money. Ask group members to give examples of the exploitation of religion today: abuses by some leaders of the electronic church, cults, and others.

Jesus came proclaiming that faith is not a transaction but a relationship. The old abuses would have to give way to a new way in religion. He said the temple of wood and stone—or material things given for salvation—is a false notion of what God requires of us. The old sacrifices are now replaced by the body of Jesus, the living sacrifice. His body, broken for the sins of the world—his body, that was to be raised in the Resurrection—is sufficient sacrifice.

The disciples and the Jews would like to have a sign that Jesus' message is authentic. But Jesus has already given a sign to them. Do they not see his mighty works every day? They stand beneath the rays of Jesus' sacrificial deeds, but they do not see them. They are like the man who stands inside a beautiful city and requests, "Show me a sign that this is a city." Or they are like the individual who, standing in the presence of God, says, "Prove to me that God exists." It is insulting to one in whose presence we stand when we presume to prove his or her existence. When taunted to prove God's existence, the early church pointed to Jesus Christ. What is our real proof of God? Many persons say Jesus Christ is the only proof we shall ever have or ever need.

One astute interpreter of events in the episode in which Jesus drove out the money changers and traders from the temple has summed up the issue of the search for signs in this way:

One has a feeling of exasperation with these people bleating for a **sign**. It seems so silly. What need of a sign when no sign merely but the thing itself is there before their eyes? How can a prophet prove that he is a prophet except by doing the deeds of a prophet, by showing the zeal and passion for righteousness that makes a prophet, by arousing people's consciences to feel as intolerable things they had never noticed, or which they dully assumed to be inevitable and woven into the make-up of life? Yet when this unknown Galilean burst suddenly into Jerusalem, and temporarily at least swept away bodily a pollution that had desecrated the temple for years, and which must have jarred the consciences of many of the more spiritual worshipers, the authorities buzzed around him, asking inane and yet natural questions. By what right are you doing this? What evidence have you that you are really sent by God and are commissioned by him? Some of them, be sure, were angry. For no reform was ever carried through without arousing opposition, often from men quite good in other ways. So, no doubt, it was here. Vested interests, they felt, were being hurt. Worshipers from other countries found it a very real convenience to have the money-changers actually in the temple precincts, ready to make the payment of their dues much simpler and more expeditious; while many would just not have imagination enough to see anything unseemly in the established way of things, or why what had been there so long should not be altered. In all which there is a warning for us.[1]

John 3:1-21. Point out that the Pharisees were among the most respected people of their day. They were the religious leaders, the elders, the most knowledgeable about temple worship and the law of Moses. Nicodemus was a leader of these people, a man blameless in observance of the law. Perhaps he was concerned that the righteousness he often saw observed was a righteousness of human beings, not the righteousness of God.

So Nicodemus, an honest seeker, comes to Jesus by night. Summarize for group members the conversation between Jesus and Nicodemus. What do they think happens in the new birth, or being born again? How do they think the new birth affects one's goals in life? one's values? What does baptism have to do with the experience of the new birth?

The participant book contains the idea that being reborn carries with it the idea of eternal life. Explore with group members what this term means in the New Testament. Christians stress their conviction that eternal life is God's gift. We do not have to die and be placed in the grave to participate in eternal life. Eternal life is a quality—God's own life—in which we participate in this life. Eternal life begins here on this earth on which we struggle. Eternal life is our sharing in God's own existence.

John's Gospel teaches us that we live in mystery. Note the conversation between Jesus and Nicodemus regarding the effects of the wind. It blows where it pleases. This blowing symbolizes the mystery that surrounds human life. We do not know how God's grace operates in the whole of our lives, but we can see its effects. All of us understand this phenomenon in our daily lives. We do not have to know all about the ways a computer system operates in order to use and enjoy its benefits. We can watch a television show or communicate around the whole world on social media, simply by pushing a few buttons or keys.

The experience of rebirth is not alone one of the intellect or of reason. The center of rebirth is the love of God extended to us in Jesus Christ and our response to that love. John's Gospel is talking about a dynamic that liberates all our powers. We sometimes ask ourselves, "What am I good for?" The correct answer is found by asking, not what we believe or hope, but what we love. The secret of Christian education lies in getting the weight of the learner's love rightly directed.

According to John's Gospel, what was the purpose of Jesus' coming down from heaven? Why can we claim that Jesus is the truth about God?

Read Numbers 21:4-9 and the paragraph in the corresponding section in the participant book on page 20 dealing with this passage. Why do you think Jesus applied this episode to his own role in the world? Why has the passage on Moses' lifting up the snake in the wilderness (John 3:14-15) become a key concept in our understanding of world salvation? Why would Martin Luther call John 3:16 "the gospel in miniature"? Why do many people today love "darkness instead of light"?

Discuss the two senses in which the word *world* is used in John. In the Prologue, the word means the created world: "the world was made through him," the world that is mentioned in Genesis 1:31. But the other use of the term means our human world, the existence of alienation where people do not know Christ. In rejecting Jesus the people are representatives of this estranged world. It is a world lost and hostile, but it is subject to God's redemption. Jesus saves this world at the same time he overcomes it.

John 3:22-36. John the Baptist had a movement all his own. He recruited and baptized disciples and preached repentance for sins. He could have been jealous of Jesus and considered Jesus an intruder into his territory. But John didn't. He rejoiced in Jesus' success, and he applauded the genuineness of Jesus' ministry. The Baptizer insisted that Jesus had come from God. John the Baptist set an example for future religious leaders to be open and gracious, supportive of genuine ministry that led people to God.

John 4:1-30, 39-42. The conversation between Jesus and a woman at Jacob's well serves to heighten the conviction that Jesus is the Savior of the world. The scene is Samaria, an area in what was the former northern kingdom of Israel. When it was conquered by Assyria in 721 BC, and the land became intermixed with other peoples and religious influences, the Hebrew religion began to change. "True" Jews felt the Samaritans were the mongrel products of foreign influence and corrupted religion. Thus the animosities between Jew and Samaritan included both racial and religious prejudice. Jesus defies the taboos and treats a Samaritan woman with compassion and respect. He goes even further in ignoring ancient prejudices against women. He listens to the woman's sad story, cutting through the prejudices against women that prevail in Samaritan and Jewish societies.

Read and summarize the discussion between Jesus and the Samaritan woman in the corresponding section of the participant book, pages 21–22. Why is the woman perplexed? What does "living water" mean to her at first? What do you think it meant to Jesus?

What does the discussion of worship have to do with the woman's life? How do we know Jesus is announcing a new day in religion? The Samaritans, according to the Jewish belief, had only had part of a legitimate religion—the Pentateuch, another name for the first five books of our Old Testament. Do you observe among Christians today this tendency to take just the pieces Scripture and tradition that confirm what we want to believe, regardless of the rest of the biblical witness? Ask group members to give some examples. What happens to the Samaritan woman? How does she come to see herself as she really is? What do class members think causes us to see reality and to change our way of life?

What does the woman of Samaria do as a result of meeting Jesus? Why do you suppose the other Samaritans in that city believed this woman's words about Jesus?

John 4:31-38. Have you ever been absorbed so deeply in your work that you missed a meal? If so, you have a small inkling of Jesus' meaning when he tells the disciples that his food is to do the will of God ("him who sent me"). Jesus' concern for God's task is total, all absorbing. It sustains his life and purpose.

Ask group members what they think of Jesus' references to the harvest. Jesus is urging his followers to go out on God's mission. They may reap a rich harvest that others have sown. The disciples have entered into the labors of others. We benefit daily from the labors of people we have never seen. We share in their labors when we take upon ourselves the work of Christ. Ask participants to cite evidences of where they have reaped because others have sown.

John 4:43-54. This story moves Jesus into Galilee, "his own country." Perhaps after all the accolades he received in Jerusalem, Jesus wants to rest and recuperate where he is not so acclaimed. But his fame precedes him, and an official—probably a Roman and a Gentile—begs him to heal his son. Perhaps wearily, Jesus answers him, "Unless you people [all of his audience, not just the official] see signs and wonders . . . you will never believe." The man asks for healing again, and Jesus grants it. The official does not rush away to check on the healing; he "took Jesus at his word."

Jews and Gentiles are involved in Jesus' ministry of healing. Jesus' signs—mighty works and miracles—always minister to human welfare. They are not given to cause a show.

DIMENSION THREE:
WHAT DOES THE BIBLE MEAN TO ME?

A New Day in Religion

Discuss these questions with group members: What does John mean by "rebirth" and "born again"?

John's Gospel stresses the idea of rebirth, not a biological experience, but a transformation of the whole person. Along with this, the Gospel emphasizes the kingdom of God, a realm one cannot enter unless one is born from above, born again. In this whole experience, the person is conscious of being the child of God, eternally loved and cherished by God.

The reality of being reborn carries the idea of eternal life. It is the reality of Jesus Christ taking charge of our affections, our wills, our lives. Through him we are reborn to new life. Through it, we are reborn, changed from self-centered creatures into persons who know our sins are forgiven and forgotten.

The symbol of all this is water (baptism), which represents cleansing. Baptism and the Holy Spirit signify the power of Christ in our lives, a power that gives victory over sin.

We then become citizens of the kingdom of God, children of God, who on this earth have life eternal—we participate in the very existence of God.

Jesus reacted in an unexpected way to the woman of Samaria. He treated her with respect and love. Are we able to treat all God's creation with this love? How do we treat the immigrant and refugee families in our neighborhoods? those whose religion, customs, or first language is different from our own? those who hold unfair prejudices toward us for any reason?

Jesus has planted the seed of this faith among us. Christians are left to reap the rich harvest. As God has sent Christ, so Christ sends us to proclaim the universal good news of God's love. Just as John the Baptist received humbly and magnificently the leadership of Jesus, so Christians today are called to serve God without pride and without jealousies, letting the credit fall where it may, but giving the final credit to God. How are you serving and giving the credit to God?

---

[1] From "The Gospel According to St. John's Exposition," by Arthur John Gossip, in *The Interpreter's Bible,* Volume 8; page 499. Copyright renewal © 1980 by Abingdon. Used by permission.

Then Jesus declared, "I am the bread of life. Whoever comes to me will never go hungry, and whoever believes in me will never be thirsty" (6:35).

JESUS THE BREAD OF LIFE

John 5–6

DIMENSION ONE: WHAT DOES THE BIBLE SAY?

Answer these questions by reading John 5

1. Where does Jesus attend the Jewish festival? (5:1)
   Jesus attends a festival in Jerusalem.

2. What happens at the pool of Bethesda? (5:2-9)
   Jesus heals a man who is an invalid.

3. How do some Jewish leaders respond to Jesus' healing on the sabbath? (5:10, 16)
   They say it is unlawful to heal on the sabbath, and they persecute Jesus.

4. Why do "the Jewish leaders" seek all the harder to kill Jesus? (5:18)
   Jesus broke the sabbath and called "God his own Father, making himself equal with God."

5. How does Jesus answer his critics? (5:19-24)
   Jesus replies that his works have been approved by God and that those who believe in God who sent him have eternal life.

6. What does Jesus say about the coming age? (5:25)
   The coming age is already at hand and now has come in Jesus.

7. Why is Jesus' judgment just? (5:30)

   Jesus came not to do his own will; he seeks "not to please myself but him who sent me."

8. What does Jesus say about the witness of John the Baptist? (5:31-36)

   John's testimony about Jesus is true, but Jesus' witness is greater than John's.

9. What witness does Jesus have that he is sent of God? (5:36)

   The work that the Father has given him to finish, and which he is doing, is Jesus' witness.

Answer these questions by reading John 6

10. Why does a crowd follow Jesus? (6:2)

    "They saw the signs he had performed by healing the sick."

11. How do the people respond when they see the sign of the feeding of the five thousand? (6:14)

    They say of Jesus "surely this is the Prophet who is to come into the world!"

12. What does Jesus do when he perceives the people want to make him king? (6:15)

    Jesus withdraws to "a mountain" by himself.

13. What does Jesus say to his frightened disciples when they see him walking on the water? (6:20)

    Jesus says, "It is I; don't be afraid."

14. When the disciples find Jesus on the other side of the lake, what is his response to their questions? (6:26-40)

    "You are looking for me, not because you saw the signs I performed but because you ate the loaves and had your fill." Jesus tells them not to "work for food that spoils, but for food that endures to eternal life." Then he talks to them about the meaning of his claim: "I am the bread that came down from heaven."

15. What is the response of "the Jews" to Jesus' words? (6:41-42)

They grumble about him and question his claim, thinking him only to be "Jesus, the son of Joseph, whose father and mother we know."

16. How does Jesus answer them? (6:43-51)

He interprets his role as "bread that came down from heaven," one who is sent by God.

17. What is the response of "the Jews" to Jesus' reiteration of his claim? (6:52)

They argue among themselves, asking how Jesus could give them his flesh to eat.

18. How does Jesus answer "the Jews"? (6:53-58)

He explains that to eat and drink of him is the means to eternal life; the living Father sent him and the one who feeds on him will live forever.

19. What do the disciples say about Jesus' words? (6:60)

They find his words are "a hard teaching" and difficult to accept.

20. What do many of Jesus' disciples do when they hear Jesus' words in verses 61-65? (6:66)

They turn away and no longer follow Jesus.

21. What is Peter's confession? (6:68-69)

He asks, "Lord, to whom shall we go? You have the words of eternal life." Peter says the disciples believe that Jesus is "the Holy One of God."

22. When does Jesus speak of Judas Iscariot? (6:70-71)

Jesus reminds the disciples that he had chosen them and that one of them is a devil.

DIMENSION TWO:
WHAT DOES THE BIBLE MEAN?

John 5:1-18. Jesus plunges into the most desperate situation, a situation from which hope seems to have departed. Why does John's story concentrate on the one man who "had been an invalid for thirty-eight years"? He wants to make clear the power of God in the situation. The man, generally presumed to have been lame, seems to have given up. He seems to be without hope. He needs a word from beyond himself and his sad plight. Jesus responds to the man's deeper need with the words, "Get up! Pick up your mat and walk."

The man has thought himself powerless and alone, but suddenly he finds himself able to walk. Jesus asks him whether he wants to be healed. In this question Jesus deals with the main issue: Would the man like to be made whole? Is he willing to drop the excuses that have hemmed him in and to face the possibility that God is working in his life? His fears and anxieties have been barriers to healing. These must be dealt with. These maladies in his existence have caused him to settle down with things as they are. The man has made himself comfortable with a second-best life, an accommodation to life as it is.

Jesus' dealing with the man breaks through this spirit of accommodation. Through a power not his own, the sick man is healed. He goes away without thanking the person who has been the instrument of his healing. He does not even learn Jesus' name. Later he learns who Jesus is and reports him to the authorities. When finally he recognizes Jesus, he is greeted with the words, "See, you are well again. Stop sinning or something worse may happen to you" (5:14). Jesus bids the man to avoid the greater enemy—sin.

What befits the sabbath? This question looms large after the healed man reports to the authorities that Jesus has healed him on the sabbath. The religious people should be asking, What goes on here? What is more important—a man's restoration to health or the observance of secondary rules? Instead, the response of the authorities is to focus on the breaking of the law.

In the moral codes of their day, the authorities had life fixed and regulated in a written code (like *Robert's Rules of Order*) that had an answer for every situation one faced. Jesus insisted that principles, not petty rules, should govern the conduct of his followers. Principles require that we think, that we see the possible consequences of values and make wise choices. We have standards to be applied reverently and wholesomely to the tough moral dilemmas that we face.

So Jesus applies principles to the matter of healing on the sabbath. One big principle: the sabbath is made for persons, not persons for the sabbath (Mark 2:27; 3:2-5). It is far better to do deeds of compassion and healing on the sabbath than to make minor rules central in our lives. Jesus tells the Jewish authorities, "My Father is always at his work to this very day, and I too am working" (John 5:17). The sabbath laws cannot apply to God. Jesus' work and God's work are one work. Jesus' followers are put on notice that their faith frees them from legalism that would give them little, simple rules for what they could or could not do in every situation. It is therefore fitting that persons do deeds of mercy and compassion on the sabbath, since God in Jesus' ministry is setting the example.

How do Christians decide on wholesome sabbath observance? Many businesses, especially retail and food service businesses are open on Sunday, and commerce seems to be brisk. Not only are stores open, we as customers keep them open. Yet we can find more biblical and faithful ways to observe the sabbath. One method is to work on our mindfulness, not simply to think of the sabbath as a time of rest. You may go to church, for example, but did you pay attention? Was your whole heart and mind focused on God and what God may say through the liturgy, Scripture, and sermon? Did you remember any of it during the week and act on it?

John 5:19-29. Review the material in the corresponding section in the participant book (pages 29–30) dealing with the claims of Jesus.

In John 5:19-29, Jesus reaffirms his oneness with God. The authorities see Jesus' claims on the level of personal divine sonship that would set Jesus above God's laws. The claims remind them of the arrogance of pagan rulers of their times who claimed divinity for themselves.

For Jesus to speak of himself as the Messiah took extraordinary and unique courage; for he knew that his words were considered blasphemy by the orthodox Jewish leaders. Jesus' statements could only divide the Jews, for Jesus' position meant that people must accept Jesus for what he said he was or reject him as a blasphemer.

Jesus, however, does not make claims according to egotistical motives. With him, every claim points to God to whom he is obedient. God delegates authority to the Son and permits Jesus to confer "life to whom he is pleased to give it." As Son of God, Jesus should be honored as God is honored. When Jesus is doing the work God has sent him to do, he should be honored as God is honored. In human affairs, we honor an ambassador from another country simply because of his or her mission.

Jesus is appointed by God to carry out the divine judgment. He has come to proclaim the future age. It is now. Judgment is present. Judgment is the crisis one encounters when Christ's message is submitted for belief or unbelief. If the person responds in faith (personal trust and obedience), the judgment is behind him or her, so that the person already lives in eternal life. Verses 28-29 apply to the future judgment and final resurrection. But the present and future aspects of judgment are present in the church.

Jesus Christ brings judgment, for a person's judgment depends on his or her response to Jesus Christ. To accept Jesus Christ is life, to reject him is death. When we accept the God of love who comes to us in Christ, we find a new relationship with God, with others, and with ourselves.

Jesus Christ raises the dead to life. This is his messianic claim. To be spiritually dead means to have given up in the struggle. Then we see ourselves as unable to overcome our faults and unable to become what we ought to be. We lose our feeling for higher things, our sensitivity to God's claims on us. We cease to repent daily—proof that we are spiritually dead. We lose our desire to learn, the challenge to use our minds, the desire to change.

In the presence of Christ we may triumph over all spiritual death. We then view with great seriousness the importance of this life, for it determines eternity. Here we choose life or death.

John 5:30-47. In these verses Jesus speaks of a number of witnesses who bear testimony to him. Who are these witnesses who confirm that Jesus has come from God? They are John the Baptist, Moses, the Scriptures, Jesus' works, and God. These are witnesses the people can believe.

Why did not more of the people believe? Many accepted these witnesses and even venerated them, and yet intellectual agreement was the extent of their "belief."

Take, for example, John the Baptist. Some who heard him described John as "a lamp that burned and gave light." They liked his preaching. They liked the sensation John had created. They applauded the movement that put John at the top of things—some would have even put John in competition with Jesus. John's role was to point to Jesus, and yet many of his admirers missed this reality.

Many of John's followers searched the Scriptures, so that the written word came to be an end in itself. The Scriptures did not point them to Jesus. Others held sacred the traditions of Moses but missed the truth to which the traditions should lead them.

Look around you and contemplate the mighty things that are happening in the name of Jesus Christ—the One whom God has sent, the One the enemies of Jesus do not believe.

The Jewish leaders clamor for absolute proof. God has given them the proof, but they will not believe the evidence before their very eyes. They are blind to the truth. Hence, they "study the Scriptures diligently." But they twist the Scriptures to prove trivial things—things that do not involve the central message of God. They pry into this and that, but they miss what God is really saying. God in the whole ministry of Jesus is trying to tell us something.

In this ministry worldly success does not come to Jesus. He does not put stock in it: "I do not accept glory from human beings" (5:41). His glory is the glory of the "one and only Son, who came from the Father" (1:14). The glory of the cross, the glory that turns the standards of this world upside down—that is the mark of the Messiah.

Verses 41-47 declare that Jesus will not be received by such people as one sent from God. And why? Jesus does not agree with them concerning the nature of God and what God is doing in the world. Many scholars say that verses 41-47 already are forecasting the shadows of the cross falling across Jesus' mission.

John 6:1-15. This miraculous feeding happens by the Sea of Galilee near Passover. Jesus feeds the physical hungers of the crowds, and yet he does more than that. He points beyond the bread to the Bread. Human beings are spiritual creatures, creatures of body, mind, and spirit, according to Christian views. They cannot be satisfied with the bread that will pass away. Like Moses, Jesus feeds the multitudes. But he does more than that; he ministers to the human yearning for God, for meaning, for full life.

The crowds, impressed by Jesus' miracles, fail to see them as signs of God's greater power. They try again to make Jesus king. He foils their efforts. What they need is not a ruler who will furnish bread and circuses. They need the abiding presence of God, a new relationship with God. Explore with group members the contrast between getting bread to satisfy daily hunger and being given the Bread of eternal life.

John 6:16-21. This passage speaks to our modem tendency to be frightened by Jesus' manifestation of his power to minister to our need. We miss the difference Jesus makes to our sense of calm and serenity. We cannot see that Jesus is in final command of the forces of nature. We live in a world where miracles have become quite ordinary, so we miss the sense of awe that the disciples experienced when they were confronted by the voice of Jesus. "It is I; don't be afraid."

Therefore, we should question ourselves. Do we worship an ordinary Christ whose power is expressed only in commonplace ways? Or do we worship the Christ of the Prologue to John's Gospel? Have modern Christians lost the sense of awe? If so, how can we reclaim that sense of awe?

John 6:22-59. In this passage Jesus speaks to the human yearning and hunger for fuller life. He tells his hearers they seek him for the wrong reason. They want the loaves and fishes to continue, and they are concerned for immediate material satisfactions. Christianity is often welcomed as a means of getting material benefits in this world. It is rejected when it is understood as an absolute obedience to God. Jesus insists again that faith is a relationship with the eternal, not a transaction over the material things of life.

Yet his hearers ask Jesus a big question about this relationship: "What must we do to do the works God requires?" (6:28). They have been given tremendous gifts and powers. God has richly endowed them with all things necessary to life. Still, they may be wasting their time on secondary things, on trivial pursuits.

Jesus answers them: "The work of God is this: to believe in the one he has sent" (6:29). Jesus' emphasis is more on being than on doing. What they are will be expressed through their doing. In John's Gospel "to believe," we remember, means to bet one's whole being on the Lord. But not everyone appreciates who the Lord is.

Jesus meets with opposition because he identifies himself with God instead of with Moses. The Jews are offended when he calls himself the bread they should eat. Eating flesh and drinking blood violated their whole tradition. Jesus' flesh and blood (the bread and wine of Holy Communion) are understood today as God's way of giving God's self to us. When we eat Christ's flesh and drink his blood, we have life by God's grace. Bread becomes more than bread—it is God's life given to us through Jesus Christ. This life is God's gift. Our salvation comes to us from above, as Jesus told Nicodemus. Faith is God's gift of sustaining power through time and eternity. Faith confers eternal life now and results in resurrection at the last day.

Why should Jesus' hearers believe in him? His coming in lowliness and love speaks to their depths. Jesus is different from all the other religious heroes they have known. He reveals the very grace and love of God. He comes teaching, reconciling, healing, suffering, and dying because this is the way the eternal God must deal with sin.

In this way Jesus gives to humankind the true bread of life. This bread, this salvation, is for all. Jesus says, "Whoever comes to me will never go hungry, and whoever believes in me will never be thirsty" (6:35). He promises his hearers that anyone who comes to him he will not cast out. Jesus declares that he is the living bread that came down from heaven. If anyone eats of this bread, that one shall live forever.

So the Christian feeds on Christ—participates in the strength of Christ, follows Christ's teaching, attains the mind of Christ, and makes his or her own the values that Christ wants in daily existence.

John 6:60-71. Not everyone is equipped and ready to follow. The disciples, hearing Jesus' proclamation, remark on how hard this teaching is to accept, and "from this time many of his disciples turned back and no longer followed him." In response, Peter makes a very early declaration of the holiness of Jesus. In sharp counterpoint to the affirmation of faith, Jesus ominously announces that one of the intimate circle will betray him. Is it at this point, perhaps, that Judas also "turned back and no longer followed" even though he remained for the time in the inner circle?

DIMENSION THREE: WHAT DOES THE BIBLE MEAN TO ME?

John 5:1-18—Do I Want to Be Well?

Review this passage again and then raise these questions. Do you need to be healed? Of what do you need to be healed? The tendency to give up? to flee from God's mercy? How does the sick man's illness differ from yours? Have you been guilty of evading a healing? What were your excuses? When have you experienced Christ's healing? Are you ready for change in your life? Are you, like the enemies of Jesus, holding on to a second-best in religion? What should be your attitude toward sabbath observance?

John 5:19-29—What Does the Messiah Mean to Me?

How might the disciples have heard all these comments about the dead hearing the voice of the Son of God and about the dead being raised? What kind of hope does that bring to you, if any, that believers are not condemned, but cross over from death to life? What do you think condemns a person?

John 6:1-5—What Does the Feeding of the Multitudes Mean to Me?

What does the story of the feeding of the five thousand say to your religious need today? What does this story say to the church today? What does your personal faith have to do with Jesus, the Bread of life?

John 6:16-21—Jesus Walking on the Water

What challenge does John 6:16-21 present to you? How do you find calm amid the storms of life? Do you really believe in the Christ who heals and commands the forces of nature?

John 6:22-71—What Does It Mean for Me to Live on the Bread of Life?

How is Christ the giver of the bread of life to you? When have you experienced him as the giver? as the bringer of judgment? What does it mean for you to live by Christ, the Bread of life?

When Jesus spoke again to the people, he said, "I am the light of the world. Whoever follows me will never walk in darkness, but will have the light of life" (8:12).

JESUS THE LIGHT OF THE WORLD

John 7–8

DIMENSION ONE: WHAT DOES THE BIBLE SAY?

Answer these questions by reading John 7

1. Why does Jesus go about in Galilee instead of Judea? (7:1)

   Jesus goes around Galilee because the Jewish leaders in Judea are waiting to take his life.

2. What do Jesus' brothers tell him to do? (7:3)

   His brothers tell him to leave Galilee and to go to Judea so that Jesus' disciples "may see the works you do."

3. When Jesus leaves for the festival and the Jewish leaders are looking for him, what do they say? (7:11-12)

   Some say he is a good man; others charge he is deceiving the people.

4. When Jesus goes into the temple and teaches, what causes the Jews to be amazed? (7:15)

   The Jews are amazed at Jesus' learning. They ask how it is that Jesus has "such learning without having been taught."

5. How does Jesus answer them? (7:16-24)

   He says his teaching is not his own but comes from God, whose honor he seeks. He reminds them that Moses had given them the law, yet they do not keep it. Jesus asks why they seek to kill him and reminds them the law of Moses condemns their desire to kill him. He asks, "If a boy can be circumcised on the Sabbath so that the law of Moses may not be broken, why are you angry with me for healing a man's whole body on the Sabbath?"

6. How do some of the people of Jerusalem react? (7:25-27)

The people of Jerusalem ask if Jesus is the man the authorities are trying to kill. They say he spoke publicly. Can it be that the authorities really know Jesus is the Christ? They say the possibility of Jesus' messiahship is denied because his origin is known.

7. What happens when the Pharisees hear the crowd whispering about Jesus? What is Jesus' response? (7:32-34)

The chief priests (Sadducees) and Pharisees (bitter enemies of the Sadducees) unite in sending the temple guards to arrest Jesus. Jesus speaks to them of his death and says that where he is going his enemies cannot come and find him.

8. What does Jesus do and say on the last day of the festival? (7:37-39)

He stands up and says loudly, "Let anyone who is thirsty come to me and drink." Jesus asserts he is the water of life.

9. What happens when the people hear these words? (7:40-44)

The people become divided over Jesus and his claims; some think he is a prophet, others the Christ. Some want to arrest him. But no one lays hands on him.

10. How is Nicodemus involved in the dispute? (7:50-52)

Nicodemus intervenes when the Pharisees argue over the crowds who are supporting Jesus. Nicodemus says the Jewish law judges no man "without first hearing him to find out what he has been doing."

Answer these questions by reading John 8

11. What happens when Jesus returns to the temple? (8:1-11)

Jesus is faced with a woman caught in the act of adultery. Jesus resolves the conflict and the charge with the statement that he does not condemn the woman. He says for her to go and sin no more and for others who would condemn her to act only if they have not sinned themselves.

12. What happens after the incident of the woman taken in adultery? (8:12-30)

    Jesus, proclaiming he is the light of the world and that he is doing the will of God, explains his mission again. The Jews dispute among themselves about the meaning of Jesus' claims. They miss his claims to oneness with God.

13. What does Jesus now say "to the Jews who had believed him"? (8:31-32)

    He tells them that if they hold to his teaching, they are really his disciples. They will know the truth, and the truth will set them free.

14. How does Jesus answer their assertion that they are free by being "Abraham's descendants"? (8:34-47)

    Jesus says, "Everyone who sins is a slave to sin." The freedom of sonship to God comes only through the Son. Though they insist that God is their father (verse 41), their murderous aim and resistance to the truth deny this and mark them as children of the devil.

15. How does Jesus answer their insults? (8:49-58)

    He says God is judge and will confirm true believers in him with eternal life. Refusal to believe, he says, cuts them off from Abraham who rejoiced in the hope of the coming Messiah. Then Jesus says, "I tell you the truth, before Abraham was born, I am!" thus claiming a preexistence and oneness with God.

16. How does this confrontation end? (8:59)

    The crowd picks up stones to throw at Jesus, but Jesus hides himself away from them and slips out of the temple.

DIMENSION TWO: WHAT DOES THE BIBLE MEAN?

John 7:1-13. Beginning on the fifteenth day of the seventh month (September-October) and lasting eight days, the Festival of Tabernacles commemorated the wilderness wanderings of the people of Israel. It was a time of thanksgiving, the celebration of rich traditions, the joys of feasting, and general merriment. By appealing to the popular fancies of the crowds, Jesus could have used the occasion to enhance his image. He had made what the crowds and the Pharisees viewed as fantastic claims for himself. Would he compromise his claims and seek the agreement and approval of the crowd?

Why did Jesus not agree to go up to Jerusalem when his brothers advised him to? His time, he said, had not come. By this he meant that the hour of God, the right opportunity, had not arrived. The time was still not right for a fuller demonstration of the divine. Perhaps Jesus was giving us a lesson in patience. We want so much to achieve our goals quickly, so we rush off without the necessary supports—prayer, discipline, study, an understanding of our problems, and a wise plan of action. We become more concerned with our public relations, with our image, than with the truth and the help of God.

When Jesus did go to Jerusalem in private, what did he find? He met with much confusion. The Jews were searching for him, most of them not knowing whom they were seeking. Some people quickly agreed he was a good man. Others thought he was "Public Enemy Number 1." They should have asked: Is he the Christ, the self-communication of God to the world, the fulfillment of human hopes and dreams, the Word made flesh and living among us?

Even Jesus' enemies asked who he was. Who is Jesus? This is still the crucial question. Discuss the identity of Jesus with group members. Why does so much depend on who he is? What is God saying to us through him? Why is Jesus loved? Why is Jesus hated? What happens when we are indifferent to Jesus' claims?

John 7:14-24. We met much of the argument carried on here in Chapter 5. The enemies of Jesus do not believe in his person—that he is the One he claims to be. Therefore, they reject his mission. The situation regarding Jesus was similar to that of a well-known person today. You know how it is for people to say, "I don't like him or her. I'll oppose what he or she stands for." Jesus' foes said that he could not have come from God.

Jesus responded to these critics with his claim made at the beginning: His teaching was not his own; it came from God. Jesus was acting on God's authority. The people should judge him by the work he was doing, not by superficial appearances. Ask class members whether they think we judge Jesus by superficial appearances. Have the appearances of evil in our world so overwhelmed us that we miss the good in our world?

John 7:25-31. Some people were familiar with Jesus' family background. To them Jesus was merely a local boy; he could not be the fulfillment of the Scriptures. To them and to many others nothing good could come out of Nazareth. The writer of John does not mention Jesus' birthplace nor the expectation that the Messiah would be a descendant of King David. The Messiah would come in a highly dramatic way, not as a poor preacher and teacher.

Others believed in Jesus because his signs were in accord with what they understood of the Scriptures. They believed because in him they encountered God. Discuss the question, Why do we believe in Jesus?

John 7:32-52. The shadow of the cross now looms over the whole mission of Jesus. The authorities would gladly arrest him and put him to death, but they fear the people. They make another attempt to take him in, but they fail. Ordered to take Jesus captive, the temple guards return empty-handed. This time they are overcome by awe in the face of Jesus' statements (7:46).

Jesus speaks according to the symbolism of the Festival of Tabernacles: Water stands for life. Without it we die. Without water life becomes impossible. Every Jew remembered the stories of how water had saved their people in the wilderness. Jesus now proclaims that he is the water of life, the very sustainer of the people's being, satisfying their deepest physical and spiritual needs.

What did the people say when they heard Jesus' promise that he is the water of life? Read verses 40-44. What would we have said?

Foiled in their attempt to arrest Jesus, the Pharisees began accusing the crowds. They expressed contempt for the crowd, showing that these people were not following the leadership of the Pharisees. They dismissed the people as an ignorant lot.

What attitude of the Pharisees have you seen in the church? Do you think Jesus approves of attitudes of contempt for the poor and the homeless? Ask class members to recall expressions of those attitudes they have seen in the newspapers or heard on radio and television.

John 7:53–8:11. Perhaps not a part of the original Gospel, this story about Jesus and his response to a helpless sinner was probably circulated in the early church. One important collection of manuscripts places this story after Luke 21:38. Many scholars think this position in Luke is the logical place for it. Read the concluding verses of Luke 21, and then read John 8:3-11. Does this story seem to fit in well? Now read John 7:45-52 and 8:12-20. Does anything seem to be missing in the sequence of events? The vocabulary of this story is different from John's, and the words used are more common to Luke's Gospel. Some editions of the Bible place John 7:53–8:11 in a footnote or identify it as a possible addition.

The important fact is that we have this precious story for our instruction. What does the story teach us?

1. *Beware of the callousness and ruthlessness of the Pharisees toward a person trapped in sin.* The religious leaders were quick to expose the woman to public disgrace. Acting from their own religious motives, they would gladly have stoned the woman to death. Their traditions and community attitudes approved their cruel intentions toward the unfortunate sinner.

2. *Beware of the temptation to use ancient law and custom to counter God's will for compassion toward sinners.* The Pharisees were locked into the past. They could not see that they and many others had a vested interest in the darkness and inequities of their time. They needed a weapon to discount Jesus, for he was a judgment on the status quo. They knew the demand for stern punishment of the woman would be popular in some circles. Yet they probably also knew Jesus was lifting a new standard against an ancient wrong.

3. *Beware of quick and unjust judgments.* The Pharisees came to Jesus evidencing quick temper and hostility. He was their real target. They wanted to trap him into an unjust judgment. But they had forgotten one thing: They, too, were sinners. The poor woman they had brought to Jesus was a member of the same human club

as they. Jesus spoke to their consciences when he wrote in the sand and placed responsibility back on them.

4. *Be ready to open your minds to the compassion of God that hates the sin but loves and cares for the sinner.* When we forget the compassion advocated by Christ, we become capable of great wrongs against his creatures. Then we forget that we too will be brought to judgment. In this way we miss the reality of divine forgiveness toward others and toward ourselves.

John 8:12-20. Jesus picked the time of the first day of the festival to announce to the people that he is the light of the world: "Whoever follows me will never walk in darkness, but will have the light of life" (verse 12b). Jesus proclaimed himself as the light of God to the world. He called the people to follow him. To walk in Jesus' footsteps means, therefore, not to go wrong. It means to have Jesus' presence and support for our lives.

We have met the images of light and darkness in our previous study (see 1:5, 9; 3:19). The images of light and darkness are familiar in Judaism. In this faith many passages of Scripture speak of God, the Torah, and the people of Israel as light. Promises of light coming into this dark world pervade the Old Testament. Psalm 27:1 proclaims, "The LORD is my light and my salvation." Isaiah 60:19 promises, "The LORD will be your everlasting light." And Micah 7:8 assures us, "Though I sit in darkness, / the LORD will be my light."

In the passage from John's Gospel, however, the author connects light and judgment. Light gives life, as when a plant denied light suddenly receives light and begins to turn green. The light is not given to judge, however, but to save. Light gives us truth, and by that light we judge ourselves. We judge ourselves when we prefer darkness to God's light. We judge ourselves by our response to the light.

So judgment comes on us when we choose darkness rather than light. To live in darkness means to lie to ourselves about our human situation. It means to refuse to hear the truth and to turn our backs on those who speak the truth.

When do we deny the light? We deny the light when we are complacent about conditions that maim human beings and make of life a dog-eat-dog existence. Darkness has overwhelmed us when we accept force, for example, as the final arbiter of human problems and disputes, when we meekly accept economic injustice in business and commerce. Darkness has taken over when we ignore prophetic voices all about us who would warn us of disasters to come.

The Gospel of John warns us against accommodating ourselves to darkness and piously calling it light. We live in a world where love is set against hatred, love is set against death, and truth stands against falsehood. By our choices we judge ourselves.

John 8:21-59. In these verses Jesus stresses the true nature of discipleship. He emphasizes the close relationship between doing and knowing the truth. Suppose a person sets out to know the truth. If, however, that person's life remains governed by greed or lust, that person is not continuing in Christ's way but in the broad way of death.

Discipleship means, then, that we base our beliefs firmly. We see how Jesus demonstrates God's love in the world, and we live our days according to God's example in Jesus Christ. We accept what Jesus teaches about God's love, about the dangers of sin, and about the purpose of our lives. Discipleship means hearing the word of God and learning it through commitment. Discipleship means that we study the word of God and build up dependable habits for our study. We do not become learners by random, haphazard approaches to faith.

Discipleship requires that we learn from Jesus—to see what he valued and how he met life's issues. Discipleship means asking ourselves, "What is God's purpose for my life?" Discipleship means coming to the point of saying, "I am not my own; I belong to Another." When we reach that point, and act accordingly, the truth has released us from fear and set us free.

The Jews rejected Jesus' understanding of freedom. They had only a partial grasp of it. For them, to be free meant to claim the Jewish birthright and to share in the Jewish tradition and law that exempted the people of Israel from slavery. Freedom? Yes, indeed, said these Jews. We have it. We are not subject to the external controls of the Romans or the Greeks. We are no one's slaves.

The Jews were descendants of Abraham. They believed this fact protected them and made them free. Jesus countered their claim. The Jews, he said, could not live on Abraham's merit. Theirs was a false sense of security. Being descendants of Abraham would not save them. They could not live off the achievements of their ancestors.

Jesus transferred the argument to a higher level. Who are the true sons of Abraham? he asked. They are those who overcome sin through the power of God. Jesus told the people to act as Abraham acted, to make God's will central in their lives. Moral stamina and spiritual sensitivity make one the true child of Abraham.

Jesus clinched his statement when he pointed to the intention of his enemies to kill him. He said these people do the bidding of their father. And who is their father? He is the devil. Jews who claim to be true children of Abraham and do not make God's will central in their lives cannot be descendants of the ancient patriarch.

In Jesus, God is confronting the people. They are being judged on their response to God's appeal to them through Jesus. When these people hate the truth and try to destroy it, they are doing the devil's work.

The enemies of Jesus now accuse him of being a Samaritan—a hated enemy. Indeed, they view him as demon-possessed and as mad with the madness of the evil one.

Jesus' assurance of who he was turned on the direct approval of God for his word and work. This word he affirmed when he said that anyone who kept his word would never see death. Jesus was here pointing to the mighty claim the whole New Testament makes: Christ is victor over our two chief enemies: sin and death.

DIMENSION THREE:
WHAT DOES THE BIBLE MEAN TO ME?

Jesus and Our Picture of Him

Jesus caused varying reactions among his fellow Jews. His brothers, for instance, reacted in a teasing manner (7:1-5). They did not believe in him as the Messiah, but they persisted in egging him on to provoke him to react. This attitude of tolerant contempt is evident in our world. We may forget that Christianity is a matter of life and death.

Hatred was the reaction of the Pharisees and chief priests to Jesus. They hated Jesus for stirring up change—change that threatened their comfortable way of life. Sometimes we love our way of life more than we love God. We hesitate to follow the sacrificial way of Christ that would lead us into change.

Those who hated Jesus sought to arrest him (7:30, 32). They had to in order to protect themselves. Our choice, if we choose to follow Christ, is to continue doing as we always have done or to do what Christ shows us to do. If our choice is not to follow Christ's direction, we must get rid of him.

Some persons met Jesus with arrogant contempt (7:15, 47-49). He did not have the right credentials in their eyes; he was not an educated rabbi, so how could he explain the law to them? We need to take great care before rejecting Jesus' teaching and love just because they do not meet our preconceived ideas. Listen to Jesus' words with an open heart and mind and be prepared to receive his love.

The crowd in Jerusalem reacted to Jesus with interest (7:11) and discussion (7:12, 43). They were interested in learning about Jesus and his message. But some folks still wondered who Jesus was and where his authority came from. Their discussion sometimes became heated.

Do similar issues today divide people about Jesus? How can we help others clarify for themselves who Jesus is?

Jesus' claim "I am the light of the world" (8:12) was an astonishing claim. The rabbis taught that the name of the Messiah was Light. So Jesus' statement was incredible to the Jews.

What does Jesus' statement mean to us? What kinds of darkness does Jesus enlighten?

"I am the good shepherd; I know my sheep and my sheep know me . . . and I lay down my life for the sheep" (10:14-15).

JESUS THE GOOD SHEPHERD
John 9–10

DIMENSION ONE: WHAT DOES THE BIBLE SAY?

Answer these questions by reading John 9

1. What do Jesus' disciples ask him about the "man born blind"? (9:2)

      They ask Jesus why the man was born blind. Did his parents' sins cause the man's blindness?

2. How does Jesus answer them? (9:3-5)

      Jesus says that the man was born blind so that God's work might be displayed in his life. While time allows we must do the work of God, Jesus says; for the night comes when no one can work. He said, "While I am in the world, I am the light of the world."

3. What does Jesus do next? (9:6-7a)

      He spits on the ground, makes mud, and places the mud on the man's eyes. Then he tells the man to go and wash himself in the pool of Siloam.

4. What happens to the man born blind? (9:7b)

      The man does as he is told, and his blindness is healed.

5. What happens next? (9:13-16)

      The man is brought before the Pharisees. They question him, and he tells them what happened. The Pharisees are not satisfied with his answer and are divided over what is happening.

6. What do the Jewish leaders do? (9:18-29)

They call the parents of the man who has received his sight and ask them about the man, but the parents say their son will have to speak for himself. The Pharisees call the man before them a second time. They question him. He cannot answer all their questions, but he stands plainly on his statement: "One thing I do know. I was blind but now I see!" This response leads the Pharisees to insult the man, saying he is a disciple of Jesus.

7. How does the man answer? (9:30-33)

The man defies the Pharisees' claim that he had been born in sin and witnesses to what Jesus has done for him.

8. How does Jesus answer all this? (9:35-38)

He confirms the witness of the man, who says he is a believer in the Son of Man.

Answer these questions by reading John 10

9. What image does Jesus use to describe himself? (10:1-15)

He declares he is the good shepherd (10:11) who lays down his life for the sheep in contrast to those who come as thieves and robbers.

10. What does Jesus say about other sheep? (10:16)

He says that he has other sheep who "are not of this sheep pen" whom he must bring also.

11. Jesus' words cause what reaction? (10:19-21)

His words again divide the Jews. Many of them say that Jesus has a demon; others ask if a demon could open the eyes of the blind.

12. What do the Jews ask Jesus in the temple? What does Jesus reply? (10:22-30)

The Jews ask Jesus to end their suspense: Is he or is he not the Christ? Jesus replies that the works he does in "my Father's name" speak for him, but the Jews do not believe. Jesus' sheep recognize his voice and follow him, and he gives them eternal life. No one can take them from him. Jesus and the Father are one.

13. How do "his Jewish opponents" respond to Jesus? (10:31)

    They take up stones to stone Jesus.

14. What does Jesus say to them, and what is their answer? (10:32-33)

    Jesus says that he has shown them many good works; for which deed will they stone him? They answer that they are stoning Jesus, not for his good works, but for blasphemy—that he, a mere man, was claiming to be God.

15. How does Jesus answer their charge? (10:34-38)

    He points out that it was written in their own law: "You are 'gods.'" They are called gods to whom the word of God came. Jesus says he has been set apart as God's Son to go into the world, he is acting on God's behalf, and he and the Father are one. He asks them to believe his works as works of God.

16. What happens then? (10:39-42)

    The Jews try to seize Jesus, but he escapes across the Jordan to the place where John had been baptizing. The crowds come to Jesus, "and in that place many believed in Jesus."

DIMENSION TWO:
WHAT DOES THE BIBLE MEAN?

John 9:1-12. Read some Old Testament passages that express the belief that the sins of the fathers are visited upon the children: Exodus 20:5b; 34:7; Numbers 14:18; Deuteronomy 5:9.

Explore with group members any questions raised by the assumption that the sins of the parents result in the afflictions of their children. What picture of God do we get from these Old Testament verses? According to Jesus, how is God related to our physical calamities? How is God's power manifested in these afflictions? Jesus sees in these sufferings the opportunity for God's compassion and grace to be shown. He sees the healing of the man born blind as a sign of his own coming as the light of the world.

Ask: Does trouble draw from you a response of courage and a challenge to realize how God's work is manifested in your life?

Why do you think Jesus warns his followers to do the work of God while there is still time? Discuss our use of time. All of us have had the experience of knowing a person who died. Later we ask ourselves. Why didn't I tell this person how much I love him or her? Why didn't I ask this person the questions that he or she alone could answer? Business people sometimes place on the walls of their offices the word NOW. Jesus warns us to value the now and to learn its urgency. What changes should we make to give priority to the relationship between Jesus and us in our daily life?

Jesus' method of healing is part of his whole self-giving that expresses the very nature of God. Jesus shares our life and meets us on the level of our daily existence. Jesus comes to us in terms of the life we know.

This principle is illustrated in *The White Nile,* by Alan Moorehead, where the author discusses the way Jesus' method prompted Dr. David Livingstone in his efforts to preach Christ in Africa.[1] For thirty years Livingstone made unceasing efforts to evangelize the African people and to bring an end to the slave trade of central Africa. Livingstone explored the unknown regions of the continent, especially as he searched to discover the sources of the Nile. His description of the massacre of helpless people at Nyangwe raised worldwide concern over the slave traffic and forced the sultan of Zanzibar to shut down the slave market on that island off Africa's east coast.

Moorehead writes that Livingstone's mission began and ended in Africa. The world-renowned doctor lived with the Africans. He ate their food, slept in their huts, and suffered the diseases and hardships the Africans endured. Livingstone once wrote: "The strangest disease I have seen in this country seems really to be broken-heartedness, and it attacks free men who have been captured and made slaves."[2]

Livingstone never lost his determination to make life better for the Africans and to end their exploitation. Moorehead says Livingstone possessed a quality that the Arabs described as *baraka,* "the power of enhancing life and making it appear better than it was before." Livingstone's mere presence seemed to have conferred a blessing upon those who met him. Even the Arab slave traders felt his spiritual quality and helped Livingstone when they could.

John 9:13-23. Review the events recorded in John 5:1-18. What common themes do you and group members find in John 5:1-18 and John 9:13-23? Why do you think so much emphasis is placed on Jesus' healing on the sabbath?

Jesus had broken the sabbath law, and for this some Pharisees were merciless. In Jewish life a person was culpable if on the sabbath he or she put out a lamp to spare the lamp or put oil in the lamp to spare the wick. A person could not walk on the sabbath wearing sandals containing nails; for the weight of the nails was a burden, and burdens could not be carried on the sabbath. Healing was forbidden on the sabbath. One could give medical help only if a life was endangered. Jesus rose above the pettiness of these rules. He put human life above excessive regulations.

Discuss the attitude of the Pharisees. They, like many people, tended to condemn any religion or any religious observance that was different from theirs. Do we sometimes hold similar attitudes?

John 9:24-34. Why did the Pharisees expel the man cured of blindness from the synagogue? What testimony of the man could they not refute? The cured man had an experience that the Pharisees could not understand. It was outside their teachings. Though the man was not educated and could not speak in theological terms, still he knew what had happened to him, "One thing I do know. I was blind but now I see!" Though the Pharisees can see, they are blind to Jesus' power. What lesson do you think the incident of Jesus' healing teaches? What does it teach us about spiritual sight?

How do you think Jesus saves us from spiritual blindness? What is our role in this salvation? Describe times when new spiritual sight took the place of your blindness.

Such spiritual blindness may strike us all. Its presence may be so subtle that we are not aware of it. A writer who was discussing an English school said in a public speech: "Students learned much about Shakespeare and Milton there, but nothing about life." A thoughtful person might respond: Poor students—they lost sensitivity to the issues of good and evil and life and death. Shakespeare and Milton *are life*. How could students be so detached and parochial that they could not see that the masters of literature speak to every age?

Ask class members to recall Bible stories in which the lives of persons were turned around because new spiritual sight came to them. Jacob at Bethel (Genesis 28:10-17), the boy Samuel's call (1 Samuel 3:1-10), Isaiah in the temple (Isaiah 6:1-8), Paul's conversion (Acts 9:1-19), Peter's vision of clean and unclean foods (Acts 10:9-16)—these and other stories may come to mind.

Think also of events in Christian history that changed a person's life. I can think of Saint Augustine's conversion in the Milanese garden, Saint Francis of Assisi's abandonment of the world to serve Christ, Martin Luther's discovery that the just shall live by faith, and John Wesley's experience in Aldersgate Street. God's revelation and light still come, in ways great and small, in all our lives; we just need eyes to see.

How do you and group members think Jesus cures our blindness?

John 9:35-41. Jesus finds the healed man and challenges him to belief in the Son of Man. Commentators have often observed that God in Jesus Christ seeks out the man who was born blind. God is the seeking God who will reach us in all the events of our experience. That encounter may involve judgment, says Jesus. "For judgment I have come into this world, so that the blind will see and those who see will become blind."

We have met the idea of divine judgment several times already in John's Gospel. Here we might stress that divine judgment has its own way of correcting situations of evil: God allows the sinner to see for himself or herself the folly of shoddy relationships and conduct. The Pharisees were anxious to find out if Jesus were talking about them. "What?" many say indignantly, "Are we blind too?" They receive the disappointing answer, "If you were blind, you would not be guilty of sin; but now that you claim you can see, your guilt remains."

Many years ago a slumlord in Los Angeles was given a thirty-day sentence to live in one of his own slum properties. The apartment was rat-infested and roach-infested. The judge decreed that the landlord should experience firsthand what it meant to live in his own building amid conditions that violated health, fire, and building code regulations.

Even without access to the details or merits of this case, it certainly seems to illustrate a principle of divine judgment. We have to live in the situations we have made for ourselves until in God's grace we are freed from them.

John 10:1-21. These verses present Jesus as the gate for the sheep. In the Middle East of Jesus' time, the sheepfolds on the hillsides were used to protect the sheep at night. The shepherd would lie down before the opening to the fold so that the sheep would have to go by him before they entered. The shepherd became the gate, for the sheep could neither enter nor go out without going over his body.

The "gate for the sheep"—this symbol pointed to the salvation of Jesus' own. Only through Jesus the gate could persons reach God. Jesus is the "way and the truth and the life"; no one can come to the Father except by him. If anyone enters through Jesus Christ, he or she will be saved. The ones who come advocating violence and trying to force their way into the fold are false leaders. These persons believe in murder and the exploitation of upheavals to gain advantages for themselves. Jesus' voice is the voice of peace, constructive reason, and compassion.

The author of John describes Jesus as the good shepherd. The Scriptures often depict us as lost sheep, and they portray Jesus as going out to seek us. The characteristic painting of this New Testament story presents God, not as one who sits upon a remote and impersonal throne, but as one who mixes in the common life we know. Jesus is the good shepherd reaching into the thorns on the wild hills to rescue the lost sheep. That is the picture of God we get from the New Testament.

Jesus knows his own—the humble ones who foster peace, love, and fullness of life. Jesus came not in war and bitter strife to bring in God's kingdom, not as the thief who seeks his own advantage.

The mark of the good shepherd is that he, unlike the hired hand, will give his life for his sheep.

Jesus' concern is not only for a small band of people of this fold. He is concerned for the world (John 3:16). The Gentiles must be brought into his Kingdom. His religion is universal—all people must be saved. First of all, Jesus comes to the house of Israel. Jesus makes clear that the revelation of God is intended for the Jews. But he is the Savior of all, one who will win the Gentiles. He speaks of one flock, who will hear his voice and for whom he will be one shepherd.

The Jews are offended and divided by Jesus' work. Some think he is mad. Others, reminded of his opening the eyes of the blind, ask whether his words can be those of a demon.

How can Christians know Christ's voice in personal and social situations? Ask group members to name some attitudes and activities that Christ would disapprove. What attitudes would Christ approve? How is Jesus the gate of the sheepfold today? How can Christians distinguish between true and false leaders?

John 10:22-42. Why do you think Jesus made his claim to be the light of the world during the Festival of Lights?

The festival grew from Jewish experiences that went back to Antiochus IV Epiphanes, the king of Syria who ruled in the period 175–164 BC. Antiochus came to his throne resolved to destroy Jewish culture and to introduce Greek thought and culture everywhere. Acting peacefully at first, he promoted Greek thought and lifestyles among the Jews. He urged the Jews to give up their religion and to become Greek in outlook. While some Jews went along with the tyrant, the people as a whole rejected Antiochus's campaign. Then the ruler attacked the Jewish people and sacked Jerusalem. According to reports of the time, some eighty thousand Jews were slain and an equal number were sold into slavery. Antiochus forbade Jews to own copies of the Law. He forbade Jewish women to circumcise their sons, and he crucified mothers who did so. Infants he slew, hanging them around the necks of their mothers.

Antiochus and his forces made the altar in the temple an altar to Zeus, turned temple rooms into brothels, and delivered the ultimate insult to the Jews: He offered up swine's flesh to the pagan divinities, a practice called to mind in the "desolating sacrilege." These atrocities stirred the Jews to revolt. The war against Antiochus was led by the Maccabean brothers who threw off the tyrant's rule in 164 BC. The Jews cleansed the temple and rebuilt its altar. Then under Judas Maccabeus they set aside a time "of gladness and joy" in celebration of their victory. The festival was variously called the Festival of the Dedication of the Altar, the Memorial of the Purification, and the Festival of Lights. Huge lights in Jewish homes and in the temple reminded the people of their hard-won freedom and that their faith had triumphed in a dark time. Their successors, the faithful Hasidim, were the forerunners of the Pharisees.

Note that the conversation in this section of Scripture focuses on who Jesus is. What does it mean to us that Jesus Christ and the Father are one?

DIMENSION THREE: WHAT DOES THE BIBLE MEAN TO ME?

John 9 and 10—Guidance for Daily Life

Jesus used a common (for that day) method to heal the man born blind. Ancient people believed that spittle, especially the spittle from certain persons and fasting spittle, had great curative power. Even today we often put a burned or cut finger in our mouth almost without thinking. Healing, after all, depends to a great extent on the patient's faith in the treatment.

By his compassion and caring attitude, Jesus gained the man's confidence and was able to heal him. We can show the same compassion and caring for those in our world who are hurting and who are outcasts. How can we apply this love and care?

What are some ways that our eyes can be opened to situations around us that need our attention? How has this happened to you?

The image of a good shepherd is one of comfort and caring. A shepherd does everything for his sheep—directs them to sources of food and water, provides a safe place for them to sleep, and searches for them when they are lost. Jesus wants to be our good shepherd. In what ways is he our good shepherd?

---

[1] *The White Nile,* by Alan Moorehead (Harper and Brothers, 1960); pages 99-119.
[2] From *The White Nile,* page 100.

"I am the resurrection and the life. The one who believes in me will live, even though they die; and whoever lives by believing in me will never die" (11:25-26).

THE RESURRECTION AND THE LIFE

John 11–12

DIMENSION ONE: WHAT DOES THE BIBLE SAY?

Answer these questions by reading John 11

1. What does Jesus say about the illness of Lazarus? (11:4)

    Jesus says that Lazarus's illness "will not end in death." The sickness is for manifesting the glory of God "so that God's Son may be glorified through it."

2. What do the disciples say to Jesus when he says they must go back to Judea? (11:8)

    They reply that the Jews have been trying to stone Jesus and question whether he should go to Judea again.

3. What does Jesus say about Lazarus's death? (11:11, 14-15)

    Lazarus, Jesus says, has fallen asleep. Then he says Lazarus is dead; and for the disciples' sake Jesus is glad he was not in Bethany when Lazarus died.

4. What do Martha and Mary do when Jesus arrives? (11:20)

    Martha goes out to meet Jesus, while Mary stays at home.

5. When Jesus sees Mary weeping, what does he say? (11:33-34)

    Jesus asks where Lazarus has been buried.

6. What does Jesus do next? (11:38-43)

Jesus, deeply moved, goes to the tomb and says, "Take away the stone." He tells them if they will believe, they will see the glory of God. When they remove the stone, Jesus prays and calls out with a loud voice, "Lazarus, come out!"

7. What is the reaction of the crowd? (11:45-46)

Many of the crowd put their faith in Jesus. Others in the crowd go to the Pharisees and tell them what Jesus has done.

8. What does Caiaphas, the high priest, tell the Sanhedrin? (11:49-52)

He predicts Jesus will die for the people. Jesus will die to save the whole nation from perishing. Jesus, he says, will not only die for the Jewish nation "but also for the scattered children of God, to bring them together and make them one."

9. What happens as a result of the Sanhedrin's meeting? (11:53)

The authorities plot to take Jesus' life.

10. What happens next? (11:54-57)

Jesus goes quietly "to a village called Ephraim" and stays with the disciples. Before the Passover the Jews come to Jerusalem for ceremonial cleansing before the festival. They ask questions and look for Jesus. Meanwhile, the chief priests and Pharisees issue orders for Jesus' arrest.

Answer these questions by reading John 12

11. What do Jesus' friends do for him when he comes to Bethany? (12:2-3)

They prepare a dinner in his honor. Martha serves while Lazarus reclines at the table with Jesus. Mary anoints Jesus' feet and dries them with her hair. She pours over them a costly pint of pure nard.

12. What is Judas's question about Mary's act? (12:4-5)

Judas wants to know why the perfume was not sold and the money given to the poor.

13. How does Jesus respond to Judas? (12:7-8)

    Jesus tells Judas to leave her alone; it was meant that this perfume be used for his burial. There will always be poor persons, but Jesus would not always be with them.

14. What does the crowd do? (12:9)

    The people gather to see Jesus and Lazarus, whom Jesus had raised from the dead.

15. What do the chief priests plan to do? (12:10-11)

    They plan to kill Lazarus. On account of Lazarus many of the Jews are going over to Jesus and putting their faith in him.

16. What does the crowd do next? (12:12-13)

    The people take palm branches and go out to meet Jesus as he approaches Jerusalem, shouting "Hosanna!" and hailing him as "the king of Israel."

17. What does Jesus do then? (12:14-15)

    Jesus finds a young donkey, sits upon it, and quotes the Scripture that he fulfills: "Your king is coming, seated on a donkey's colt." (See Zechariah 9:9.)

18. What is Jesus' response to the questions of the Greeks? (12:23-26)

    Jesus says the time has come for him to be glorified. He says, "Unless a kernel of wheat falls to the ground and dies, it remains only a single seed. But if it dies, it produces many seeds."

19. How do various ones, including Jesus, respond to the voice from heaven? (12:29-32)

    The crowd standing by say it thundered. Others say that an angel spoke to Jesus. Jesus says the voice came for the people's benefit, not for his. He says his death will judge the world and defeat the devil ("the prince of this world"). When Jesus has been lifted up from the earth, he says he will draw all people to himself.

20. Why do many not believe in Jesus despite his signs? (12:37-41)

    John points out that the unbelievers are confirming the words of Isaiah. As in Isaiah's day, the people are being blind and hard-hearted.

21. Why do others not express a belief in Jesus? (12:42-43)

They fear the authorities may put them out of the synagogue, and they love "human praise more than praise from God."

DIMENSION TWO: WHAT DOES THE BIBLE MEAN?

John 11:1-16. The Resurrection is the central theme of the whole Gospel of John. Begin the session by asking class members why the discussion of the Resurrection recurs throughout the whole Gospel. Ask various class members to read aloud these verses from John: 5:25-29; 11:24-26. Then ask why they think John's discussion of the Resurrection is centered in the story of a single human being, a man named Lazarus, whose name means "God has helped." This individual is chosen for a great sign that points to the greater manifestation of God.

Share this summary of the New Testament teaching on the Resurrection with the group members.

- The New Testament assumes Jesus Christ's resurrection from the dead. The resurrection of Jesus was the work of God, confirmed in the lives of redeemed sinners and in the rise of the church to power and victory from the ashes of defeat.
- The earliest New Testament witness to Jesus Christ's resurrection may be the affirmation of 1 Corinthians 15. Here Paul related the resurrection of Christ to the resurrection of believers. The heart of the gospel is found in the great act of God in raising Jesus from the dead.
- To deny Jesus Christ's resurrection means to abandon the gospel. Stressing the corporate nature of our human existence, Paul believed that just as all persons share in the death of Adam, so those who live "in Christ" will share in the life of Christ eternally. The belief in our resurrection and God's act in raising Jesus Christ stand together.
- Paul discussed the kind of body we will have after our resurrection; he concluded that it will be a "spiritual body." In Paul's view, the body can be both physical and spiritual, a body of flesh and a body of spirit. Though the body of flesh dies, the body of spirit is raised to eternal life. Thus Paul believed the individuality and continuity of the person is preserved. Paul did not accept the Greek concept that a radical division exists between body and soul. He did not lose the uniqueness of the individual by submerging the person in some vague spirituality or some other impersonal essence. The resurrection of Jesus Christ affirms that the individual is raised up to share in eternal life with Christ.

- Jesus Christ's resurrection is a mystery. The Resurrection is God's mighty act for our salvation, an act that we cannot fully understand but something we can accept through faith in, personal trust of, and obedience to Christ. The Resurrection was Christ's victory over sin and death.[1]

The events recorded in John 11:1-16 have their basis in the Incarnation. These events are likewise based in God's eternal love, on God's mighty acts of redemption.

God "proves" God by doing what is true to the divine nature. Our modern habit is to look for the "proof" of God by looking to the immensities of space, the wonder of the stars, predictable sequences in nature, and the ordering of all things by God's foresight and power.

John 11:17-37. The friends of Jesus are grieving for Lazarus when Jesus arrives in Bethany. Jesus comes to them as the final resurrection. He brings the assurance that fellowship with God is possible here and now. Jesus tells them that eternal life, with an entirely new quality—a new hope—is possible now.

Life is dismal indeed when the Christian hope is lost. What do we miss when we no longer have the assurance of the Christian hope of eternal life? Theologian Emil Brunner has dealt with this question in his book *Eternal Hope*.[2] Among the consequences to us when hope in eternal life is lost are these:

1. *Panic fear of the end.* Having lost the peace that faith in eternal life gives, the individual seeks to find meaning in the scramble for material goods, for wealth, and for sensual gratification of immediate desires. Life becomes purposeless, so that the person asks: When the doors threaten to close and all seems over forever, why not lose oneself in immediate preoccupations? Life is aimless, and we have so little time. Let us eat, drink, and be merry while the rat race lasts.

2. *The tendency to nihilism.* Nihilism is the viewpoint that traditional values and beliefs are unfounded and that human life is senseless and useless. In society the idea takes hold that all morals and ethics are relative and that human society can find a substitute for hope in eternal life. So the idea emerges that belief in human progress can take the place of this hope—that belief in progress can take the place of the kingdom of God. Accordingly, the loss of the hope of eternity demolishes the value of the individual. Human life becomes very cheap if we do not believe there is a world beyond this present one. Often we make purely temporal ideas absolute, and our tendency is to ascribe an absolute value to the race, the tribe, the political and social system, in place of faith in God.

3. *The concealment of death.* When we no longer see the person as destined for eternal life—as one everlastingly precious to God—a great sense of emptiness steals into our lives. Death marks the end of the individual's life. So we deceive ourselves about death and its finality. Often death is reported in the newspapers in ways that try to soften its harsh reality. A person does not die; he or she passes away.

4. *The absolute valuation of natural vitality,* that is, "the brutal justification and operation of the will in power." When the restraints on persons that belief in the afterlife gives are withdrawn, then people are ready for totalitarianisms of the worst sort. Sheer human power-grasping is recognized as permissible. It can "make itself absolute and unleash itself in boundless ferocity." Humanity took that step, Brunner says, in the absolutism of Marx, Lenin, and Stalin.

This then is Brunner's summary of the results of the loss of faith in eternal life. Ask group members why we become contemptuous of persons when our faith in eternal life is lost. Do they believe that life breaks up when people do not believe in eternal life anymore? How have they seen this break-up happen?

John 11:38-44. Jesus gave three directions at Lazarus's tomb: "Take away the stone," "Lazarus, come out!" "Take off the grave clothes and let him go."

What are the stones that keep us entombed today? Guilt for past sins? Worries and cares? Fears? Lack of trust in God?

Jesus speaks to our dead selves. He becomes "the resurrection and the life" to us when we are dead in our sins and dead to God. The parable-like story of Lazarus is certainly an educational event for us all.

How would you describe the true environment of persons—the true home of the human spirit? What does it mean for us to be called to be human? How can we "come out to life"?

John 11:45-57. Jesus' sign of raising Lazarus from the dead causes people to take action. "Many of the Jews" believe in Jesus. They accept this sign as pointing to his messiahship. Other Jews, however, go directly to the Pharisees and tell them "what Jesus had done." Why did Jesus' words and actions produce divisions among the people? What are ways Jesus' words and the action of Christians produce divisions in our world?

Immediately the Sanhedrin is called together to decide what they shall do about Jesus. The Council members are afraid of losing their favored position of authority under the Romans. What was Caiaphas's prophecy?

The tension is thick in Jerusalem as the Jews gather for the Festival of the Passover. They look here and there for Jesus. "What do you think? Isn't he coming to the festival at all?" This verse may have been used in the early church as preparation for celebrating Holy Communion. As often as we fail Christ, will he still come to our Communion feast? Christ always remains faithful to us though we are faithless to him.

The danger is growing for Jesus. The chief priests and Pharisees are asking for anyone to inform them of Jesus' whereabouts "so that they might arrest him."

Why did all eyes turn toward Jerusalem at the time of the Passover? Read Exodus 12:1-28. This passage is an account of the Festivals of Passover and Unleavened Bread. The Jews valued these festivals very highly. The stories of the festivals can act for Christians as a parable of the whole existence of humankind. Of their own free will the Jews went down into Egypt. There the Jews became enslaved until God used Moses for their deliverance. Just as the Jews were delivered from slavery by Moses, so the human race is delivered from sin and death by Jesus Christ.

John 12:1-11. Focus now on the story of the anointing of Jesus' body for burial. Some persons still see Mary's act as impractical and wasteful. Jesus was able, however, to recognize and accept Mary's impulsive act as a spontaneous outpouring of her gratitude for all Jesus meant to her. To be able to accept graciously is a difficult thing for most of us to do. Yet Jesus saw beyond what we may see as an embarrassing moment to Mary's affectionate heart. In the Gospel of Matthew's account of this event, Jesus says, "She has done a beautiful thing" (Matthew 26:10).

Note in the Gospels of Matthew and of Mark (Mark 14:3-9, which is almost word for word the same) this person is identified simply as "a woman." No hint at all is given as to her character or where she came from. The Gospel of Luke (Luke 7:36-47) places the story very early in the text, uses the anointing story to set up an object lesson for the host about forgiveness, says nothing about the poor, and identifies her as "a woman who lived a sinful life." Nowhere is this woman identified as Mary Magdalene, although tradition has suggested it was she. In fact, John has identified her as Mary, the sister of Martha and Lazarus; a fine, upstanding member of a very respected family. On one point all the Gospels agree—Jesus thinks the woman did a good and proper thing, and she has been immortalized for it.

The story may suggest to some persons the relationship between worship (Mary's act of anointing Jesus' feet) and Christian service (giving to the poor). How do you see that relationship working in your church? How does the Judas spirit make itself known today? Would the love that prompted Mary's deed ever neglect the needs of the poor?

John 12:12-19. Jesus enters Jerusalem riding on a young donkey, thus fulfilling the prophet Zechariah's prophecy that the Messiah will arrive "lowly and riding on a donkey" (Zechariah 9:9). Riding on a donkey indicates that Jesus comes in peace. (Riding a horse indicates the rider is bent on war.) Jesus is coming as the Prince of Peace, not as the warrior king most Jews are expecting.

Why do you think Jesus now shows himself dramatically as the Messiah? How does Jesus reverse the standards of this world? What do his actions imply for Christians today? What might our attitudes toward the values and institutions of contemporary culture be? Give some examples of how Christians are reversing the success and power standards of this world.

John 12:20-36a. Jesus' public ministry is drawing to a close. To the Greeks who come seeking Jesus, he speaks some hard words: "Anyone who loves their life will lose it." Jesus is telling of his own death and of how his followers must approach life. Only because persons have been willing to face death have great ideas lived. Only when we bury personal ambitions can we serve God.

What kind of glorification does Jesus now face? Jesus' glorification will come at his crucifixion. Why would Jesus first pray to be saved from this hour? Most people do not want to die, especially when they see more challenges to be met in life. Obedience does not come without cost. Why must Jesus go to the cross? Jesus knows that his obedience in going to the cross will deal a deathblow to Satan. The sign of Jesus raised up on the cross will draw all people to Jesus.

John 12:36b-50. John quotes verses from the prophet Isaiah. These verses seem to say that our unbelief is due to God's action, that God has chosen some people to believe and others not to believe. Surely the God that Jesus taught about would not be so arbitrary.

William Barclay points out that a basic belief of the Jews was that God is behind everything. Nothing can happen outside the purpose of God. When a person does not accept God's message, God can still achieve God's purpose. God can use our unbelief for God's purposes.[3]

People find various reasons for not believing in God. Some of the Jews heard Jesus and believed him but would not confess it for fear of retaliation from the Pharisees, that "they would be put out of the synagogue; for they loved human praise more than praise from God" (12:42-43).

In his final words to the general public, Jesus repeats the claim that is basic to his life and teaching: In Jesus we are confronted with God. Jesus came into our world to save us. God's love

sent Jesus, not God's wrath. Yet through Jesus' words we will be judged, the more so if we have heard his words and have not followed him.

DIMENSION THREE:
WHAT DOES THE BIBLE MEAN TO ME?

The group may discuss the following topic or use the material in the participant book.

The Resurrection and the Life

"I am the resurrection and the life. The one who believes in me will live, even though they die; and whoever lives by believing in me will never die" (11:25-26).

Jesus' words surely do not speak of our physical death; even Christians die physical deaths. Jesus was speaking of death to sin. In our selfishness we are dead to the needs of others. In our insensitivity we are dead to the feelings of others. In our petty dishonesties we are dead to honor. These deaths can be overcome, and we can receive new life when we hear Jesus' words and heed them.

Our new life brings us into a new relationship with God and with life. The new relationship with God brings us freedom. As we lose our fear and know absolutely that God is love, we are more open to live life as Jesus has commanded. Life becomes a lovely thing, and we have no fear of dying and going to live another life with God and Christ.

In what ways, if any, does a belief in a life to come affect how you regard and act in the present? How does belief in resurrection impact our selfishness, insensitivity, or dishonesty?

Many of us may claim that we are not afraid of death because of the promise of eternal life, but most of us would very much prefer to put off dying. Or, to say it another way, we aren't afraid of what comes after the moment of death, but passing out of this life can entail suffering, pain, and misery; both our own and of those we love. How do you sort out your feelings about end of life and life after life?

---

[1] Excerpt from "A Pauline Wordbook," by Woodrow A. Geier in *Paul: Leader's Guide*; pages 137-38. Copyright© 1987 by Graded Press.

[2] From *Eternal Hope*, by Emil Brunner, translated by Harold Knight (Westminster, 1954); pages 91-94.

[3] From *The Gospel of John*, Volume 2, revised edition, by William Barclay (Westminster, 1975); pages 132-33.

"Peace I leave with you; my peace I give you. . . . Do not let your hearts be troubled and do not be afraid" (14:27).

7

THE WAY AND THE TRUTH AND THE LIFE

John 13–14

DIMENSION ONE: WHAT DOES THE BIBLE SAY?

Answer these questions by reading John 13

1. What does Jesus know that gives him the power and the will to wash the disciples' feet? (13:3)

    Jesus knows that God has put all things in his power, that he has come from God and is returning to God.

2. What does Jesus do before the Passover Festival? (13:4-5)

    He gets up from the supper table, prepares himself, and washes the disciples' feet.

3. What does Simon Peter say when Jesus comes to him? (13:6-9)

    Peter says that Jesus will never be allowed to wash his feet; but in response to Jesus' words, Peter asks Jesus to wash him all over.

4. How does Jesus answer Peter? (13:10)

    Jesus tells Peter that a person who has bathed is clean and "needs only to wash their feet."

5. What does Jesus say after he finishes the washing? (13:12-16)

    He resumes his place and tells the disciples he has just given them an example of how they should treat one another. "No servant," he says, "is greater than his master."

6. What does Jesus say about his disciples? (13:17-20)

"Now that you know these things, you will be blessed if you do them." Jesus says he knows whom he has chosen and that "he who shared my bread has turned against me" so that the Scriptures may be fulfilled. Jesus says that when anyone receives a disciple, that person is receiving Jesus and the God who sent him.

7. How is the betrayal of Judas Iscariot presented? (13:21-30)

Jesus is troubled after speaking with the disciples. He says one of them will betray him. "One of them, the disciple whom Jesus loved" (probably John), asks Jesus to tell who the betrayer is. Jesus replies that the one to whom he gives the piece of bread when it has been dipped is the betrayer. He gives the bread to Judas and tells him to do quickly what he will do.

8. What does Jesus say about the glorification of God and of himself? (13:31)

"Now the Son of Man is glorified and God is glorified in him."

9. What counsel does Jesus give to his disciples? (13:33-35)

"You will look for me: . . . Where I am going, you cannot come." Jesus gives them a new command to love one another. Their love should be founded on his love for them. They are Jesus' disciples if they have love for one another.

10. What does Simon Peter ask? (13:36a)

Peter asks Jesus where he is going.

11. What is Jesus' reply? (13:36b)

Jesus says Peter cannot come now but that later he can follow.

12. What does Jesus say to Peter when the disciple vows to lay down his life for Jesus? (13:38)

Jesus tells Peter that the disciple will disown him three times before the rooster crows.

Answer these questions by reading John 14

13. What assurances does Jesus give to the disciples? (14:1-21)

"Do not let your hearts be troubled." "The words I say to you I do not speak on my own authority. Rather, it is the Father, living in me, who is doing his work." Jesus speaks of the place he has prepared for them and that he will come back to take them there. Jesus says he is "the way and the truth and the life. No one comes to the Father except through me." He says he and the Father are one. Anyone who believes in Jesus will do the works that he does and even greater works. Jesus says the Spirit of truth will be in his followers: "I will not leave you as orphans; I will come to you." Anyone who keeps Jesus' commandments out of love will be loved by the Father.

14. What additional assurances does Jesus promise? (14:25-31)

God will send the Holy Spirit to be with the disciples. The Spirit will teach them all things and remind them of everything Jesus has said to them. Jesus will leave his followers with a peace that the world cannot give; so they should not be troubled or afraid. Jesus tells the disciples these things before they take place so that they may believe.

DIMENSION TWO: WHAT DOES THE BIBLE MEAN?

John 13:1-20. Chapter 12 describes the close of Jesus' public ministry. Now comes a lull in activity while Jesus is instructing his disciples about the meaning of his coming. He does this in the upper room and under serious threats against himself and his disciples. Jesus has shown the disciples that he is the way and the truth and the life; but now he wants to emphasize the meaning of these terms.

The disciples are at supper. During the meal, Jesus, who "knew that the Father had put all things under his power, and that he had come from God and was returning to God" (13:3), rose from the table, prepared for the washing, and began to wash the disciples' feet.

In the Gospel of Luke, a dispute arises among the disciples as they are traveling toward Jerusalem and this meal. "A dispute also arose among them as to which of them was considered to be greatest" (Luke 22:24). Perhaps this dispute led to Jesus' actions at the meal.

Since the roads in Palestine were either dirty in dry weather or muddy in wet weather, most homes kept a jar of water and a towel near the door. The sandals people wore were merely a sole held on the foot by straps, giving little protection against the dust or mud. As each visitor to a home arrived, a servant or family member washed the visitor's feet. Perhaps the disciples were still so engrossed in their dispute that no one would accept the duty of arranging for everyone's feet to be washed.

Here Jesus teaches the disciples and us a significant truth about ourselves. When we know where we come from, we are free persons. We are no longer orphans. We no longer feel lowborn. We no longer are under the evil power of the threat of being destroyed by insults and humiliations. We live in God's world, and we are free to serve God's creatures. We know from where we have come; we know to whom we shall return. Ours is no longer a craven existence.

Explore with class members the meaning of Christian freedom. Many counselors trace the spiritual maladies of individuals to an unawareness of who they are. We do not love God, nor do we love others, because we do not like ourselves. Our image of ourselves is distorted, faulty. We cannot cheerfully assume menial tasks for Christ.

Christianity speaks a message of true self-esteem. Christ is not concerned to buck up a false image of us. Left to ourselves, we are unlovely; but we share in the love of God. God values each of us with a love that is everlasting.

Who then is greatest in the kingdom of God? This question persists in the Gospels. In the upper room Jesus demonstrates the answer. To be eternally loved by God means to be free to serve: to be released from the slavish idea of competition, dominance, and superiority.

Simon Peter was at first enamored of worldly ideas of success and power. He vied for top recognition. Peter insisted on a total washing of himself, but he soon drew back from this possibility. Why did Peter change his attitude? What do you think about the total and deeper cleansing of baptism and participation in Jesus' movement? Are we Christians able to accept the baptism of Christ? What does that baptism involve? How do we respond when deep trouble comes? when we face hardships and sacrifices? Ask a group member to read aloud Mark 10:35-45. Then ask participants to give their views on true greatness.

John 13:21-30. When the disciples were told that one of them would betray Jesus, they began to look perplexedly at one another. "Who, me?" each said in effect.

Judas had been picked by Jesus for special honor (John 13:29 says he was the disciples' treasurer), and yet Judas violated Jesus' trust and turned his Lord over to the authorities.

"And it was night." The connection between Judas's deed and the fall of night makes for a powerful symbol. Is there something of Judas in each of us? When have we felt we have betrayed the truth?

What ultimately happened to Judas? Christians like to speculate about this question, but we do not have the answer. Matthew 27:3-5 and Acts 1:15-19 tell two different accounts of what happened to Judas. Review these passages along with others you have identified from the Gospel of John to get a composite picture of the kind of man John finds Judas to be. What does the Scripture tell us about Judas's plight? What kind of judgment falls on Judas? How does he suffer? What do you think about the solution to Judas's agony?

John 13:31-38. Now Jesus' hour has come. "Now the Son of Man is glorified." Jesus' glory comes at the cost of his life. The greatest glory comes from the greatest sacrifice. We remember Albert Schweitzer, not because he was a brilliant musician, theologian, or mathematician. We remember him because he sacrificed any success and fortune he may have gained in these fields to give his life to help people in Africa who did not have a doctor. Martin Luther King, Jr. insisted on standing up to the powers of racism, injustice, and violence to preach peace with justice, and was slain for his efforts. He was warned of danger, yet served jail time and ultimately gave his life for something greater. While the sacrifice may not require death, many people find tremendous spiritual bravery to stand for God in spite of danger. Who do you know who loves and gives sacrificially?

In Jesus, God is glorified. Through his complete obedience to God's will, Jesus gave supreme honor and glory to God.

Humans cannot know and love a Being who remains aloof and untouchable. Through the Incarnation and through Jesus' death on the cross God has shown God's glory in allowing us access to God. Now we know that God is love and understands our sorrow and pain.

God will also glorify Jesus. Though death on the cross was Jesus' glory, God demonstrated that glory in the Resurrection. Jesus' humiliation was changed to victory.

Even as he faced death, Jesus gave his disciples one last commandment: to love one another. Jesus' love for the disciples was selfless, sacrificial, understanding, and forgiving. Though they could not know all these facets of his love, Jesus held the disciples up to the best that they could be. He challenged them and us to follow his example and to love one another.

John 14:1-14. Why can we characterize this passage as the expression of calm in the midst of the gathering storm? Why can Jesus say, "Do not let your hearts be troubled"? Recall occasions when these words have been meaningful to you.

What kind of place has Jesus prepared for us? It is a place, not of separation, but where we realize divine love is incarnate in Christ. In this love Christians know that heaven is where Jesus is. It means that we enjoy even in the most bitter circumstances the assurance that Jesus' promises are true.

"No one comes to the Father except through me." What is Jesus' answer to Thomas's question? How do we know the way? Is this way the only way for anybody and everybody, or is it the only way for those who claim to follow Jesus Christ? Do you think that events at the Last Supper tell us what the way is like?

What is Jesus' answer to Philip? How do you think experiences with Jesus help us know God? We gain knowledge of God (verses 8-11) only through the person, work, and words of Jesus; and through prayer we may do even greater works than Jesus has done (verses 12-17). What might those greater works be? How would we do even greater works than Jesus?

Discuss Jesus' words, "You may ask me for anything in my name, and I will do it." Does this mean all prayer will be answered? What does it mean to ask for something in the name of another? What prevents some of our prayers from being answered? How do we know when our prayers are in Jesus' name?

John 14:15-31. From beginning to end, Jesus has sought to inspire courage in his followers. He who has loved these people to the end constantly reminds them that God is seeking deepened fellowship with God's children.

How will this be achieved? Jesus will pray to the Father, and God will send the Holy Spirit to live with the disciples and with us forever. The Spirit will be the prime reality for Christians, but the world will not be able to recognize his presence and his works among us and in the world. Why will the world be unable to recognize the work of the Holy Spirit?

Jesus recognized that the world could not see the Holy Spirit because the world was not equipped with the finer vision of God's love. We may illustrate this truth by referring to the vision of experts. A skilled medical doctor who works to heal persons who have dread diseases may spot trouble in a person's health that the layperson would miss. A skilled diamond cutter may see a precious jewel in a rough stone that a lay observer could rarely see and certainly not attain.

Can you remember times when you did not recognize the Spirit? What attitudes must we have to recognize the Spirit?

Our fellowship with Christ depends on love that results in obedience (verses 25-27). The Spirit helps us recall and understand Christ's teachings (verse 26) and brings peace to us (verse 27). Jesus promises that he will not leave us bereft or desolate. The Holy Spirit is a living presence with us always.

"Peace I leave with you; my peace I give you. I do not give to you as the world gives." What kind of peace does Christ's love give us? How does it differ from the peace of the world? The Hebrew word for peace, *shalom*, does not mean simply the absence of trouble. *Shalom* refers to all things that lead to our highest good. This peace we cannot lose; it is independent of outside influences.

DIMENSION THREE: WHAT DOES THE BIBLE MEAN TO ME?

John 13:1-20—Jesus as Servant

Jesus' example of servanthood is a strong picture. Just prior to their last meal together, the disciples had been arguing about who was the greatest among them. Status is very important to us, even from a young age. When teams are being picked on the playground at school, we want to be recognized as a good player by being picked first, and all players want to be included and regarded as an asset to the team.

Even among church leaders pride of place, of status, is important. The mission of the church cannot be carried forth because a committee member did not get elected chairperson and refused to cooperate with the other committee members. A choir member does not get to sing a solo and refuses to sing at all. A generous contributor insists on decisions that please the giver and holds the congregation hostage in fear of losing the income. Jesus is teaching the lesson that only one kind of greatness exists—that of service.

John 13:21-30—Betrayal

No one among the disciples suspected that Judas planned to betray Jesus, although John apparently did not trust him (12:4-6). No one tried to stop Judas from leaving the meal on this last night. But Jesus knew. And even though Jesus knew what was in Judas's heart, he made appeal after appeal to Judas not to do this evil deed.

At the meal, Judas was placed on Jesus' left, the place of honor. In this place Jesus could talk intimately and privately with Judas without the other disciples overhearing. Jesus also offered Judas a special tidbit at the meal. In the Eastern world offering the first morsel at a meal was a special honor.

Nothing touched Judas's heart that night. He turned his back on Jesus, going out into the night. Following Christ is to walk in the light. To turn our back on him leads only into darkness. When have you walked in the darkness by denying Christ? How do you see the light when you are following Christ?

John 14:1-7—"The Way and the Truth and the Life"

In becoming our "way," Jesus does not just give us directions to follow—he walks with us, showing us the way to go. How can we find our way with Jesus?

Teaching the truth and being the truth are not the same thing. Most of us know what the truth is, but few of us are always truthful—little white lies to save someone's feelings or to smooth over a tense situation often pop out of our mouths. Only Jesus could say, "I am the truth." How can Jesus as the truth help us in meeting the moral questions of our life?

Jesus alone can show us how to make life worth living. We are searching for life, not knowledge about life, but that which will make life worth living. How does Jesus give our life this meaning?

John 14:27—"My Peace I Give to You"

The world offers us the peace of escape. This peace means the avoidance of conflict, the refusal to face things. Jesus offers us the peace of conquest. It is a permanent peace, not depending on events in the world. Nothing can separate us from Jesus' peace. How can we find this peace? How do we keep it?

"In this world you will have trouble. But take heart! I have overcome the world" (16:33)

8

JESUS THE TRUE VINE

John 15–16

DIMENSION ONE:
WHAT DOES THE BIBLE SAY?

Answer these questions by reading John 15

1. What images does Jesus use to begin Chapter 15? (15:1-6)

    He speaks of himself as the true vine; of God as the gardener (or vinedresser); of the Father's care for the vineyard so it will bear good fruit; of the disciples as the branches; of the unity that should exist among God, Jesus, and the life of faithful believers.

2. What happens to the branch that bears no fruit? (15:2, 6b)

    The gardener cuts off every branch that bears no fruit and burns it.

3. What happens to every branch that bears good fruit? (15:2)

    It is trimmed so it can bear more fruit.

4. What is the duty of the disciple? (15:4-7)

    The disciple's duty is to remain in Jesus and retain Jesus' words in himself or herself.

5. What happens if the disciples keep Jesus' command? (15:10)

    The disciples will remain in Jesus' love.

6. Why has Jesus spoken to his disciples of these things? (15:11)

    He has spoken of these things that his joy may be in them and that their joy may be complete.

7. What is Jesus' command? (15:12)

   Jesus commands the disciples to love each other as he has loved them.

8. When are the disciples no longer called servants, but Jesus' friends? (15:14-15)

   The disciples become Jesus' friends when they do what he commands.

9. Why did Jesus choose the disciples? (15:16)

   Jesus chose the disciples so that they could bear fruit that will last.

10. Why does the world hate the disciples? (15:18-19)

    The world hates Jesus' disciples because the world hates Jesus, who has chosen them.

11. What will the Advocate do when he comes? (15:26)

    The Advocate will testify about Jesus.

Answer these questions by reading John 16

12. Why has Jesus told "all this"? (16:1)

    Jesus has told "all this" so the disciples "will not fall away."

13. What will happen to the disciples? (16:2)

    The disciples will be put out of the synagogues; they will be persecuted; and they will be killed.

14. Why will these frightful things be done to the disciples? (16:2b-3)

    These frightful things will happen because people will think they are offering service to God and because the world has not known the Father or Jesus.

15. Where is Jesus going? (16:5)

    He will return to God who sent him to the world.

16. What will be the role of the Holy Spirit? (16:8-15)

    The Holy Spirit will convict the world of guilt in regard to sin and righteousness, and of judgment. He will also guide the disciples into all truth and will glorify Jesus.

17. What does Jesus mean by the words "a little while"? (16:16-22)

    Temporary sorrow over Jesus' death will yield to joy over Jesus' resurrection and abiding presence.

18. What will Jesus' pledge of triumph do? (16:25-33)

    Jesus' pledge of triumph will make clear all Jesus' teachings, reveal the love of God, empower the disciples' prayers, and offer peace amid trouble.

DIMENSION TWO: WHAT DOES THE BIBLE MEAN?

John 15:1-17. List on a chalkboard or poster paper the images that Jesus uses to begin Chapter 15. Why do you think Jesus uses the figure of the vineyard that appears in various places in the Old Testament?

Ask class members to read Isaiah 5:1-7; Psalm 80:9-15; Jeremiah 2:21; Ezekiel 15; and Hosea 10:1. In John 15:1, Jesus connects the church, the New Israel, with these images of the vineyard in the Old Testament. Jesus is now fulfilling the Old Testament promise of God's redeeming activity.

A healthy vine requires careful tending to promote wholesome, orderly growth. Often a gardener may turn his or her back on the vineyard for a while only to discover that the vines have grown wild. But in the case of the present vine, the New Israel, God is the gardener or vinedresser. Jesus is the vine. The disciples constitute the branches.

Discuss what it means to be branches of the vine, which is the source of life. What does Jesus mean when he says, "Remain in me"? How do we remain in Jesus? Like the branches of a lush vine, says Jesus, my followers must remain closely attached to the source of their life. They must always remember from where they have come and where they are going.

How is the church renewed? By private prayer and prayer groups? by public worship? by frequent celebration of Holy Communion? In many churches some members stay away from the service of Holy Communion. What do they miss in the Christian life? List the reasons for regular attendance at Holy Communion. By their nonattendance, how are Christians neglecting the central reality of their faith?

The church is renewed by faithful study of the Bible and books on the Christian faith. Does your church maintain an attractive library containing books essential for understanding the

Christian faith? Is the library easily accessible to all? Discuss ways your group can improve the library and its use.

Jesus speaks of sending the disciples out to represent him in the world. So the church is renewed by serving others—visiting the sick, caring for widows and orphans, ministering to prisoners and to persons who are poor or homeless. Jesus sends us out to bear witness to him in society. Discuss ways Christians are witnessing to Christ today.

John 15:18-27. The Romans had a tremendous passion for discipline and order. They controlled a vast empire that stretched from the British Isles to the Euphrates River and from North Africa to Germany. The empire's lands included people of all kinds of races and religions. How could the Roman government hold the various elements together so that order could be attained? Without order nations cannot endure.

The Roman rulers were tolerant of religions so long as the religions could prove their beliefs and practices were not a threat to the state. The Romans could accept all gods. But Jewish monotheism and the Christianity that grew from it were suspect from the start. They were seen as troublemakers for the well-ordered state.

The Roman rulers needed a unifying force that would transcend the ambitions, loyalties, and conflicts of the various peoples subjected to Rome. They found this unifying force in emperor worship. This worship developed from the peoples of the empire themselves. The masses derived great benefits from Roman order. These people needed common symbols of meaning and patriotism that would hold the empire together. Caesar worship provided these symbols.

At first reluctant to be reverenced as gods, the rulers later found Caesar worship to be the force that could weld the empire into unity. Caesar worship could work to provide order, peace, and prosperity if all groups would acknowledge the emperors as gods. After all, the imperial rulers represented the spirit and the meaning of Rome. So emperor worship stood for the gratitude of various peoples for what Rome had done to achieve a peace that embraced the world. The Roman rulers allowed the various peoples to worship their own gods, but they insisted that all persons had to acknowledge Caesar as supreme. The Caesars eventually required every individual to burn incense to the emperor as a sign of loyalty to the state. Subjects of Rome were required to burn incense and to affirm, "Caesar is Lord."

The Christians refused to put the emperor above Christ. Christians, they declared, could not agree to worship what was human and finite. Not Caesar but Christ was their Lord.

The refusal of Christians to worship Caesar brought the serious charges of the Roman authorities. Christians were denounced as dangerous and unpatriotic. They were under suspicion of the Roman populace and the imperial powers. They were suspected of working to undermine the state.

What were some of the objections to the Christians? What were some atrocities charged to them? The populace of the Roman world readily accepted stories that accused Christians of cannibalism, a suspicion that sprang from the words of the Christian's private meal: "This is my body, which is for you" and "This cup is the new covenant in my blood" (1 Corinthians 11:24-25). Their enemies also accused the Christians of sexual immoralities growing out of the love feast or weekly meal. Christians greeted one another with "a holy kiss" or kiss of peace, and their foes read into their acts the charge that the Christians were engaging in immoral sexual practices.

The Christians were also charged with setting fires. Under the emperor Nero, they were charged with the terrible fires that ravaged Rome in AD 64.

To add to all these charges the public spread tales that the Christians were desecrating their marriage vows, breaking up families, and dividing homes. There was some truth in this last charge; for sometimes a child was rejected because he or she became a Christian, and sometimes half the members in a household became Christians while the other half remained in their non-Christian religion. All the divisions made for tension and disunity in the family.

William Barclay (in *The Gospel of John*, Volume 2; Westminster, 1975) sums up an excellent discussion of why the world hated the Christians by saying that the world suspects people who are different—the world keenly dislikes people whose lives condemn it. But the basic demand on the Christian is that he or she have the courage to be good.

Christians lived by higher standards than their neighbors around them. Their faith increasingly became a criticism of the low standards and conduct of the general population. Though Christians had the courage to be different, this courage would be punished. The world could not tolerate their idealism and their living on the basis of faith, hope, and love. Their admirable conduct was a constant criticism of their society.

In the upper room Jesus warned his followers that they would be persecuted, precisely because the world—a human society organized in disregard of God—was built of sin and would resent people who held to higher standards of living. Jesus represented the need for thorough cleansing from sin that only loyalty to God can bring about.

Jesus told his disciples that dire calamities would fall on them, but that he would not leave them bereft of help. He would send to them the help of the Holy Spirit or Advocate who would be a constant witness to God's love and care. They in turn would be required to witness to the world out of their personal experiences.

In *The Different Drum*, M. Scott Peck, a Christian psychiatrist, describes some means Christians adopt to "take matters that are properly related to each other and put them in airtight compartments." One example he cites is of the businessman who attends church services regularly on Sunday mornings, thinks he loves God, thinks he loves God's creation and his neighbors, but who has no problem with his company's dumping of toxic wastes into streams near his business. Here is the way Peck discusses the problem of integrity.

- *Integrity is never painless.* It requires that we let matters rub up against each other, that we fully experience the tension of conflicting needs, demands, and interests, that we even be emotionally torn apart by them. Take, for example, the fact that this country, on whose coinage is written the words "In God We Trust," is also the leading manufacturer and seller of weapons in the world. What are we to do with this? Should we be perfectly comfortable about it? Should we keep these matters in separate compartments? Or should we wonder if there is a conflict between them and agonize over the tension of trying to resolve that conflict? Should we consider, for instance, with integrity, changing the inscription on our coinage to read "In Weapons We Trust" or "In God We Partially Trust"?

- Since integrity is never painless, so community is never painless. It also requires itself to be fully open, vulnerable, to the tension of conflicting needs, demands, and interests of its members and of the community as a whole. It does not seek to avoid conflict but to reconcile it. And the essence of reconciliation is that painful, sacrificial process of emptying. Community always pushes its members to empty themselves sufficiently to make room for the other point of view, the new and different understanding. Community continually urges both itself and its individual members painfully, yet joyously, into even deeper levels of integrity.[1]

In his book *Training in Christianity,* Søren Kierkegaard, a Danish theologian, wrote (using male-centric, rather than inclusive language) about Christ drawing all persons to himself:

From on High He will draw all unto Himself.

- *From on high*—for here upon earth He went about in lowliness, in the lowly form of a servant, in poverty and wretchedness, in suffering. This indeed was Christianity, not that a rich man makes the poor rich, but that the poorest of all makes all men rich, both the rich and the poor. And this indeed was Christianity, not that it is the happy man who comforts the afflicted, but that it is He who of all men is the most afflicted.—He will draw all to Himself—*draw* them to Himself, for He would *entice* no one. To draw to Himself truly, means in one sense to repel men. In thy nature and in mine and in that of every man there is something He would do away with; with respect to all this He repels men. Lowliness and humiliation are the stone of stumbling, the possibility of offence, and thou art situated between His humiliation which lies behind, and the exaltation—this is the reason why it is said that He draws to Himself. To entice is an untrue way of drawing to Himself, but He would entice no one; humiliation belongs to Him just as essentially as exaltation. In case there was one who could love Him only in His exaltation—such a man's vision is confused, he knows not Christ, neither loves Him at all, but takes Him in vain. Christ was the truth [in His humiliation] and is the truth.[2]

John 16:1-21. Jesus' dealing with us shows a plan and a method. He knows our pace in learning, and he sets the method of teaching to fit with our possibilities. "I have much more to say to you, more than you can now bear." When we think back over our lives, we realize that some learnings we could not bear at the time. We have to master simple arithmetic and be at home with simple numbers and fractions before we can tackle the binomial theorem. Jesus teaches through experience, helping us comprehend his will and purpose as we are able. Christianity will engage us in constant growth, using all our powers and helping us become ever more mature disciples.

For our learning, Jesus will send the Holy Spirit who will instruct us in all things. The Spirit is not just for believers who receive his message. He will come to save and heal the whole world.

The Spirit will "guide you into all the truth," glorify the Christ, and "will tell you what is yet to come." The Advocate will reprove the world of sin because it rejected the Christ. He will reprove the world of judgment. Convicting the world on these scores, the Advocate will contend with the world so that it will be challenged to repudiate its bad decision to crucify the Christ.

Evil will not have the last word; for the Crucifixion will be seen as victory over sin and death, not as the disgrace Jesus' enemies would label it. Jesus' passion, death, and resurrection will complete the revelation of the incarnate Word—a truth the disciples are now called upon to accept and proclaim to the world.

John 16:22-33. Now is your time of grief, but I will see you again." I will see you again—We use these words in common, everyday speech to say that our relationship with another person is not over. It will continue into the future. Jesus reminds us that no matter how sorrowful life may become, no matter how many personal sorrows and failures, no matter how obvious it would seem that evil has triumphed in the world, he will see us again.

Jesus is going to the cross, a journey that in the world's eyes will be a sorry end to his strange venture with the human race. But the cross is the way back to God, who sent Jesus on our behalf. Each of us can say now that Jesus the Christ will see us again. Because he sees us again, we can take joy in life; for it is redeemed by him. The joy is from inward to outward—that is why no one can take it from us. It will not be held captive by the world of change and threat.

"In that day you will no longer ask me anything." We are frustrated and sometimes embittered by the unanswered questions and unsolved problems that haunt us. These are here as divine challenges. We live in mystery, and the mystery prompts us to ask questions. But in Christ's kingdom we shall see God. We shall have full understanding.

"Ask and you will receive, and your joy will be complete." By going to the cross, Jesus has established for us a new relationship with God. In that relationship and in Christ's name, we are as children who are free to make our requests known. God will hear our requests. God will respond to them according to our needs and God's purposes for us. Always we should remember to pray, "Your will be done."

"I have been speaking figuratively." Jesus has used figures that are hard to understand, sayings that are veiled to the outside world, figures that prompt the Christian to think. Jesus has been speaking to us in figures—remember the bread of life, the water of life, the good shepherd, the light of the world, and others? But now Jesus speaks more plainly. We can now grasp the language of the cross in Jesus' words. This language is directed at us and at every human being. The language is clear; everyone can understand it; it is the language of sacrificial love. Certainly no one has ever spoken more clearly. Jesus is the personal expression of the love of God to us.

"Now you are speaking clearly and without figures of speech." Jesus has revealed to us the glory of God. God has sent to earth his very heart!

We believe God is speaking plainly in Jesus Christ, speaking in the call to us to be faithful to the Son of Man, the Son of God.

"Do you now believe? . . . A time is coming . . . when you will be scattered . . . [and] will leave me all alone. Yet I am not alone, for my Father is with me." Jesus bids us beware lest we desert him when the going gets tough. On that night in Jerusalem the disciples were put to the test. We are tested daily. Let us pray for divine aid that we may be faithful. We are prone to leave Jesus alone, to believe at the moment when it is popular and safe to believe. Is our faith strong enough to endure in times of upheaval and terror?

"I have told you these things, so that in me you may have peace." Jesus gives the peace of God, the peace that the world cannot give. The world wants the peace of selfishness, of conformity to its low ambitions and standards; but Jesus gives us another peace. His peace is like the peace that possessed the man who built his house on the rock. It will stand.

"In this world you will have trouble. But take heart! I have overcome the world." Jesus looks down into the future, knowing that in a world like ours tribulation will inevitably come. He sees disaster for the disciples, and at the same time he envisions the courage that he will send his own by the Holy Spirit. So his great gift to us is courage. We worship a Savior who promises he is more than a match for what evil can do to us.

"Take heart! I have overcome the world."

DIMENSION THREE: WHAT DOES THE BIBLE MEAN TO ME?

The group may discuss the following topics or use the material in the participant book.

John 15:18-27—Jesus' Warnings of Persecution

The Christian life is a costly business. We should ask ourselves to what extent we are bearing the costs of Christ's witness. Few Christians in America are persecuted for their faith, but we should examine our attitudes and conduct to see whether the reason is because we are making compromises with the world. Would your neighbor recognize you as a Christian just by observing your day-to-day conduct?

Review the section on John 15:18-27 in the participant book. Summarize Jesus' warning of persecution and his references to what was happening in the world ruled by Rome. How was the world's hatred of the Christians being expressed? How is it expressed today? How does the world express its hatred for God? In daily life it sometimes happens that men and women show contempt for God by mistreating God's children. How do you think Christians may be partly responsible for this mistreatment? How do we ignore Christ's people? What can we do to change these attitudes that hurt people?

Discuss the meaning of Jesus' words in Matthew 25 and how there he identifies with the unfortunate people of earth. Who are the "least of these" in our world? How are Christians ministering to them? Søren Kierkegaard wrote: "Everyone knows his neighbor at a distance, and yet it is impossible to see him at a distance; if you do not see him so close at hand that, before God, you see him conditionally in every man, then you do not see him at all."[3]

How do we see our neighbor "at a distance"? Seeing him or her at a distance may mean seeing him or her impersonally as we would see an object, not a human being. Could seeing our neighbor "at a distance" mean also neglecting to bear witness against evils that maim our neighbor?

Discuss the relevance of emperor worship as it seeks to achieve purpose and meaning. Do modern people engage in "emperor worship"—making and giving ultimate allegiance to that which is human and finite? What are some of our modern gods? The state? patriotism? society? material gain?

Why must Christians refuse to put patriotism and loyalty to the state above their loyalty to Christ? How is the Christian faith a criticism of the society in which we live today? What are some areas of our nation's life in which Christians can bear witness for Christ? Unrestrained consumerism? sexual immorality? exploitation of sex and violence in the communications media? violence and corruption in commercial sports? pollution of the environment? the arena of increasingly uncivil discourse?

John 16:1-24—A Little While of Sorrow

Jesus stressed to his disciples that the persecutions would be severe, but that they would be a preface to the joy that would come to his own. Read to group members John 16:16-24. Discuss the nature of the consolation Jesus promises the disciples. Ask group members what they think Jesus is saying about our need for a comforting faith.

---

[1] From *The Different Drum*, by M. Scott Peck, M.D. (Simon and Schuster, 1987), page 235.

[2] From *Training in Christianity and the Edifying Discourse Which Accompanied It,* by Søren Kierkegaard; translated with an introduction and notes by Walter Lowrie (Princeton University Press, 1944), pages 153-54.

[3] From *Works of Love,* by Søren Kierkegaard (Princeton University Press, 1946), page 66.

"My prayer is not that you take them out of the world but that you protect them from the evil one" (17:15).

JESUS' PRAYER OF ADORATION AND THANKSGIVING

John 17

DIMENSION ONE: WHAT DOES THE BIBLE SAY?

Answer these questions by reading John 17

1. What does Jesus do before the disciples leave the upper room? (17:1a)

   Jesus prays what has become known as the high priestly prayer.

2. What is Jesus' first petition? (17:1b)

   Jesus says, "Father, the time has come. Glorify your Son that your Son may glorify you."

3. Of what does glorification of the Father consist? (17:2)

   God's glorification consists in the giving of eternal life to all whom God has given Jesus.

4. Of what does eternal life consist? (17:3)

   Eternal life is found in the knowledge of the only true God and of Jesus Christ whom God has sent.

5. How has Jesus glorified God on earth? (17:4-6)

   Jesus has glorified God by doing the work God has sent him to do and by revealing God's name to the disciples whom God has given to Jesus.

6. Why does Jesus pray for the disciples? (17:9-11a)

    Jesus prays for the disciples for three reasons: (1) because they belong to God, (2) because Jesus is glorified in them, and (3) because the disciples will soon be left without the counsel and protection of Jesus when he returns to God.

7. What is Jesus' prayer to God on behalf of the disciples? (17:11b)

    Jesus prays that God will protect them by the power of God's name and that they will be one, as God and Jesus are one.

8. What has Jesus given the disciples? (17:14a)

    Jesus has given them the word of God.

9. Why has the world hated the disciples? (17:14b)

    The world has hated the disciples because "they are not of the world any more than I [Jesus] am of the world."

10. What more does Jesus pray for? (17:15-17)

    Jesus prays, not that God should keep the disciples out of the world, but that God should "protect them from the evil one." He prays that God will sanctify them in God's truth.

11. For whom does Jesus now pray? (17:20-23)

    Jesus prays for all those who will believe in him in the future that they may be brought to complete unity.

12. How does Chapter 17 close? (17:25-26)

    Chapter 17 closes with Jesus' words that the world has not recognized God, but that he and the disciples have known God who has sent Jesus into the world. Jesus also says that he has made known God's name, and that he will continue to make it known. Finally, Jesus prays that the love with which God has loved Jesus will be in the disciples and that Jesus will be in them.

DIMENSION TWO:
WHAT DOES THE BIBLE MEAN?

John 17: An Overall View. Prayer was an essential part of Jesus' life. Though he rebuked mere formalized prayers (Matthew 6:5-8), he gave us the Lord's Prayer to use as a model (Matthew 6:9-13). Jesus' example to us shows how important prayer was to his life. He rose early for prayer (Mark 1:35). After feeding the five thousand Jesus went off alone to pray (Matthew 14:23). At his baptism Jesus was praying when the Holy Spirit "descended on him" (Luke 3:21-22). Jesus was in prayer all night before choosing his closest followers (Luke 6:12-13). In the Gospel of Luke we learn that Jesus was praying as the Transfiguration took place (Luke 9:28-29). It was prayer in the garden of Gethsemane that prepared Jesus for his suffering (Luke 22:41). And Jesus' last words from the cross were a prayer (Luke 23:46).

Fittingly, then, Jesus' last words to his disciples come in the form of a prayer. Ask group members to share their views on what prayer means to them.

In his classic book entitled *Prayer*, George A. Buttrick describes again and again Jesus' attitude toward prayer and his way of prayer. Jesus prayed, Dr. Buttrick says, in aloneness and in comradeship. He prayed "in the routine day" and "under provocation of crisis." Dr. Buttrick continues:

- Of the seven "Words of the Cross" three and perhaps four are prayers. The prayer of pardon, "Father, forgive them, for they know not what they do," leaves us "defenseless utterly." This vigil of prayer, never closely described in the Gospels, but repeatedly mentioned and reflected, is an ungainsayable testimony. He prayed and prayed—in the "great congregation" of the Temple, in the local friendship of the synagogue, in the circle of his friends, on the housetop under Syrian stars, in the fields outside Jerusalem, on the lonely mountainside, in the "inner chamber"—until prayer became the climate of his days. The saints said that "to work is to pray," and they believed profoundly that "to pray is to work." Jesus said in the language of deeds that "to live is to pray," and that "to pray is to live."
- We must not dogmatize about the limits of prayer, though we must recognize certain limits and try to trace them. For instance, we cannot too quickly conclude from Jesus that petitionary prayer has no place. Yet the fact remains that Jesus asked nothing for himself except daily bread, strength in the testing, and grace to reveal God to the world.[1]

This lesson is devoted to a single prayer of Jesus, a prayer that sums up his life and ministry. In this prayer Jesus prays for himself, but he asks nothing for himself (verses 1-5). He is concerned with the will of God alone. Jesus prays for his disciples (verses 6-19) that they be strengthened for God's tasks, that they remain faithful, and that they be kept in God's care and protected from the evil one. Jesus prays for the universal church and for us who belong to it (verses 20-26). Jesus wants his followers to be united with him. Unity is the main theme of Jesus' discourses on the night of his arrest.

John 17:1-5. The great climax of God's redemptive purpose is at hand. The time for Jesus' glorification and for his glorification of God has arrived.

What does it mean to glorify something or someone? Our dictionaries can suggest common meanings: to make glorious by bestowing honor, praise, or admiration; to elevate to celestial glory; to shed radiance or splendor on (as a large chandelier glorifies the entire room); to cause to have great beauty, charm, or appeal; to give glory to (as in worship); and many other meanings.

In the Old Testament, the "glory of God" is a term used to indicate that which the Jews can comprehend, by sight originally, of God's presence on earth. The idea goes back to Moses when God came down in the pillar of cloud and entered the tent of meeting to talk with him face to face, while the cloud stayed outside the door. The people saw the cloud as the visible sign of God's presence (Exodus 33:7-11), so that the cloud came to be a symbol of the divine presence. It was also seen as a veil to obscure the brilliance and power of the divine presence. Why was this so? Except in rare instances, the cloud veiled God's glory from human vision; for it was said that a human being could not endure the full light of God's presence and live.

The central meaning of divine glory is one of weight and substance that commands respect and honor. Glory stood for strength and power, brightness, wealth, honor, dignity, and noble bearing. For God's enemies, the glory of God was a devouring fire. When the Jews began to look forward to the messianic age, the glory came to be thought of no longer as the actual or possible experience in this life but as a characteristic of the messianic age. Slowly the glory turned *eschatological*—that is, pointing to the end times.

In the New Testament, the glory becomes an essential part of the kingdom of God. Present then, it was also expected in the future. Its eschatological factors converged dramatically in Jesus Christ. The glory of God shone around the shepherds when the angels sang at Jesus' birth. Jesus had made known the glory of God, for the people grasped the meaning of the divine glory through Christ. Christ is proclaimed as the glory of God available to all who have eyes to see. The Fourth Gospel stresses stronger than do other writings the full biblical content of the word *glory*: "We have seen his glory, the glory of the one and only Son, who came from the Father" (John 1:14b).

In his miracles Jesus revealed his glory (2:11), a glory not of human beings but of God (5:41; 17:5). The high priestly prayer is dominated by the idea of God's glory. Jesus will go to the cross, not as a pathetic martyr, but as victorious sovereign over all life. Jesus' passion and resurrection reveal to the utmost the glory of God.

This brief summary of the concept of God's glory should help you grasp the deeper meaning of the glorification of Jesus and of God that we see centered in the high priestly prayer. Why is the cross central to Jesus' glory? How does it reveal God? How does the cross finish the work that Jesus was sent to do? Why does the cross appeal to many of us in the twenty-first century?

The cross glorified God because it was suffered in obedience to God. Jesus could have evaded the cross, but he could not have glorified God by the evasion. Jesus honored God by obedience. Just as a child honors a parent by obedience or as a citizen honors his or her country by obedience, so Jesus honored God by doing God's will.

Examine the concept of Jesus to the effect that he was not of this world. Contrast worldly glory with that of the cross and the kingdom of God. What are the characteristics of the glory of this world? Money? fame? power? prestige? notoriety?

How did God answer Jesus' prayer that the Son be glorified? Why do we say the cross was Jesus' way back to God? The cross and the Resurrection freed Jesus from the limitations of time and space. He could now be present over the whole earth and be available to everyone.

John 17:6-19. "I have revealed you to those whom you gave me." Jesus has told us what God is like. To manifest his glory God dwells in lowliness. God comes to us in Jesus Christ. In "A Death in the Desert," a poem on John's Gospel, the English poet Robert Browning has described God's revelation this way:

> Though the whole earth should be in wickedness,
>
> We had the truth, might leave the rest to God.[2]

The Incarnation has made known clearer than anything else ever has that God is in the world that "the divine power first made."

> Is not his love at issue still with sin,
>
> Visibly when a wrong is done on earth?
>
> Love, wrong, and pain, what see I else around?
>
> Yea, and the Resurrection and Uprise
>
> To the right hand of the throne—what is it beside,
>
> When such truth, breaking bounds, o'erfloods my soul
>
> And, as I saw the sin and death, even so
>
> See I the need yet transiency of both,
>
> The good and glory consummated thence?
>
> I saw the power; I see the Love, once weak,
>
> Resume the Power; and in this word "I see,"
>
> Lo, there is recognized the Spirit of both
>
> That moving o'er the spirit of man, unblinds
>
> His eye and bids him look.[3]

Browning went so far as to say that the acknowledgment of God in Christ will solve all problems. He wrote:

> I say, the acknowledgment of God in Christ
>
> Accepted by thy reason, solves for thee
>
> All questions in the earth and out of it.[4]

There is much truth in what Browning says, but the Gospel of John stresses more than the acknowledgment of Jesus Christ by our reason. The revelation of God in Jesus Christ is directed to the whole person—mind, body, and soul. It grasps us in our total existence. Belief in Jesus Christ means commitment. Jesus not only tells us about the love of God, he imparts this love to us. What does it mean for Jesus to manifest the name of God? Do Christians today manifest God's name? How?

The Gospel of John says much about the unity of the church. This unity is grounded in our common love of God in Jesus Christ. It is strengthened by the realization that we are all one. God makes us one by God's work in creation and redemption.

What do group members think of Jesus' vision of the unity of humankind? What does the prayer tell us about Jesus' expectations for the future of his followers? Why does any person's death diminish us? How does Jesus expect us to be involved in humankind?

Jesus knew his disciples would face a hostile world when he left them, but he would send the Holy Spirit to be their counselor and guide.

Why did the world hate the disciples? Why are many Christians hated today? Why do you think Jesus would not pray that God take the disciples out of the world? What is the lesson for Christians and the church in this? How does a Christian witness to Jesus today? Ask group members to give some examples of Christian witness they have observed. What do they think is the most effective Christian witness?

What does it mean to be consecrated? Why did Jesus put emphasis on consecration (sanctification) of the disciples? How do you think Jesus Christ equips us for his witness today? Mention some persons you know—in the church and out—who are fitted with special skills for witnessing to God's love and justice today.

John 17:20-26. These verses that close Jesus' high priestly prayer show his complete faith and confidence in God and in the future for his followers. The immediate future is certainly grim for Jesus and his small band of followers. The next day Jesus is crucified. His followers become depressed and scatter around the country. Jesus looks beyond this grimness to a glorious future where many people will come to follow him.

Jesus' prayer for these latter-day followers (including us) is that they all will be one as he and God are one. The unity Jesus is praying for is a unity of personal relationship, not an administrative or organizational unity. Christians differ greatly in the ways they organize and administer their individual churches. But the love of God for each of them never changes. Jesus prays that this same love will be present in Christians' interpersonal relationships also. How are your class members working toward this unity of relationship with God and with other Christians?

Jesus ends his prayer by speaking of his coming glory. His glory will be the cross. By his perfect obedience to God's will, Jesus is glorified. We, too, can find glory in suffering for and being obedient to God's will. Why is being obedient to God's will often a difficult task? Why does our obedience sometimes lead to suffering?

DIMENSION THREE:
WHAT DOES THE BIBLE MEAN TO ME?

The group members may discuss the following topic before closing with using the meditation in the participant book.

John 17—Jesus Prays for Us

Read John 17 aloud, perhaps in more than one Bible translation. Ask participants to list their feelings about the prayer as they listen to it, remembering these are Jesus' last words to his disciples. Do they agree that these are the best words Jesus could have left as his final message? Are there other messages Jesus could have left as his final message? Are there other messages Jesus could have left with the disciples? What are they?

Since most American Christians do not have to face the kinds of persecution that Jesus describes that his disciples will have to face, what meaning do these words have for us? How can contemporary Christians find comfort in Jesus' prayer?

Use the meditation in Dimension Three of the participant book as your closing for this session.

---

[1] From *Prayer*, by George A. Buttrick (Abingdon Press, 1947), pages 36-37.

[2] "A Death in the Desert," by Robert Browning, in *The Complete Poetic and Dramatic Works of Robert Browning* (Houghton Mifflin, 1895), page 387.

[3] "A Death in the Desert," page 387.

[4] "A Death in the Desert," page 390.

"You say that I am a king. In fact, the reason I was born and came into the world is to testify to the truth" (18:37).

JESUS IS ARRESTED

John 18

DIMENSION ONE: WHAT DOES THE BIBLE SAY?

Answer these questions by reading John 18

1. Where does Jesus go after he finishes the conversation with the disciples? (18:1)

    He goes with the disciples across the Kidron Valley, where there is a garden, which they all enter.

2. What does Judas do? (18:2-3)

    He goes to the garden with a detachment of soldiers and officials from the chief priests and the Pharisees.

3. How does Jesus respond to the coming of this detachment? (18:4)

    He steps forward and asks who they want.

4. What happens then? (18:5-8)

    When Jesus identifies himself, the crowd draws back and falls to the ground. Jesus asks again, "Who is it you want?" They ask for Jesus of Nazareth and he tells the band, "I told you that I am he." He asks them to let his disciples go.

5. What does Simon Peter do? (18:10)

    Peter draws his sword and strikes Malchus, the high priest's servant, cutting off the man's right ear.

6. How does Jesus react to Peter's action? (18:11)

He tells Peter to put away his sword and asks, "Shall I not drink the cup the Father has given me?"

7. What happens then? (18:12-14)

The soldiers and officials seize Jesus, bind him, and lead him to Annas, the father-in-law of Caiaphas, the "high priest that year."

8. What does Simon Peter do now? (18:15-16a)

He follows Jesus to the court of the high priest and stands outside the door of the court.

9. What does the girl on duty at the door say? (18:17)

She asks Peter, "You aren't one of this man's [Jesus'] disciples too, are you?"

10. What does the high priest do? (18:19)

He questions Jesus about his disciples and his teaching.

11. What does Jesus tell him? (18:20-21)

Jesus says he had taught openly in the synagogues and in the temple, where all Jews assembled. The high priest, Jesus says, should question those persons who had heard him.

12. What does one of the officials do after Jesus replies to the high priest? (18:22)

He strikes Jesus in the face.

13. What does Annas do now? (18:24)

He sends Jesus, bound, "to Caiaphas the high priest."

14. What happens to Peter, and how does he respond? (18:25-27)

Twice more those in the high priest's courtyard accuse Peter of being a disciple of Jesus, and twice more he denies the charge.

15. Where do the soldiers and officials now take Jesus? (18:28)

    They take Jesus to the palace of the Roman governor (Pontius Pilate).

16. What does Pilate do and say? (18:29)

    Pilate goes out to meet the band of accusers and asks, "What charges are you bringing against this man?"

17. How do they answer Pilate? (18:30)

    They say they would not have brought Jesus to Pilate if Jesus had not been a criminal.

18. What is Pilate's response? (18:31a)

    He tells them to take Jesus and judge him by their own law.

19. What do the Jews say to this? (18:31b)

    They reply that they "have no right to execute anyone."

20. What now happens between Jesus and Pilate? (18:33-38a)

    Pilate has Jesus brought before him. He asks Jesus if he is the king of the Jews. He also asks what Jesus had done that his own Jewish nation had brought him to trial. Jesus replies that his kingdom is not of this world. Pilate answers, "You are a king, then!" Jesus responds that Pilate is right in saying so. He has come into the world, Jesus says, to testify to the truth. Everyone who listens to him is on the side of the truth. Pilate asks, "What is truth?"

21. What does Pilate now tell the Jews? (18:38b-39)

    He tells them that he finds no basis for a charge against Jesus, but that according to Jewish custom he can release one man to the Jews at the Passover. He asks if they want him to release Jesus.

22. What do the Jews say to this? (18:40)

    The Jews shout out that they want Pilate to release not Jesus but Barabbas, who had taken part in an uprising.

DIMENSION TWO:
WHAT DOES THE BIBLE MEAN?

The Passion Narrative. When we speak of the Passion narrative, we mean the events of the arrest, the trial and Crucifixion, the burial, the discovery of the empty tomb, and Jesus' appearances to the disciples. This narrative is recorded by Matthew, Mark, Luke, and John, who tell the same story but differ here and there in their use of episodes and descriptive details concerning Jesus. They all bear witness to the life, death, and resurrection of Jesus Christ. All agree that in Jesus the eternal God has said something very special to the human race. The Gospel writers also have their own individual concerns, and scholars generally agree that the Fourth Gospel's author is especially concerned with theology.

In *The Interpretation of the Fourth Gospel* (Cambridge University Press, 1965), a detailed study for scholars, C. H. Dodd discusses six traits of the Synoptic narratives (Matthew, Mark, and Luke) that are not included in the Fourth Gospel's Passion narrative (Chapters 18–21). They are listed here:

1. Generally, John's Passion narrative does not include the wonders occurring in nature that the others report. For example, the darkening of the sun in Mark's account (Mark 15:33); the earthquakes accompanying the Crucifixion and Resurrection in Matthew (Matthew 27:51b; 28:2); and the healing of the servant's ear as recorded in Luke (Luke 22:51).

2. John fails to give a eucharistic (Holy Communion) quality to the Last Supper, but that theme is included in the story of the feeding of the multitude (John 6:1-14).

3. John does not include the story of Jesus praying in Gethsemane (Matthew 26:36-46; Mark 14:32-42; Luke 22:39-46, at the Mount of Olives).

4. John says nothing of the charge of blasphemy lodged against Jesus in the high priest's court or of Jesus' confession at the same occasion that he was the Messiah (Mark 14:60-64). These charges do appear in the section of John's Gospel describing Jesus' signs, however (John 10:30-39).

5. John does not include Mark's report that the cross was carried by Simon of Cyrene (Mark 15:21), reporting that Jesus carried the cross alone (John 19:17).

6. John does not refer to mocking and reviling of Jesus on the cross (Matthew 27:38-44; Luke 23:35-37). John omits Luke's account of expressions of sympathy from the women of Jerusalem (Luke 23:28-32) and from one of the crucified robbers (Luke 23:39-43). John leaves out Jesus' cry of abandonment on the cross (Matthew 27:46; Mark 15:34), a cry that Luke omits also.

Dodd also lists some fifteen instances where John includes details not given by Matthew, Mark, and Luke. Some examples are given here:

1. John stresses the voluntary character of Jesus' suffering. In the garden when the soldiers hesitate to arrest him, Jesus gives himself up—doing so on condition that his disciples be allowed to go free (18:7-8).

2. John lays greater emphasis on the political charge against Jesus by the Roman court. John de-emphasizes the importance of the hearing in the Jewish court.

3. John stresses the innocence of Jesus (18:38b; 19:4, 6b) more than Mark, but not more than Luke.

4. John includes the incident of the mother and the beloved disciple (John 19:26-27), which no other Gospel writer reports.

5. In chronicling the Crucifixion, John submits a different set of prophecies fulfilled. He cites "They divided my clothes" (John 19:24), an episode to which the other Gospels only allude. Other prophecies that do not appear in Matthew, Mark, and Luke are "I am thirsty" (19:28), "Not one of his bones will be broken" (19:36), and "They will look on the one they have pierced" (19:37).

6. John includes the detail that immediately upon the death of Jesus a thrust of a spear in his side brought forth water and blood (19:34). He draws special attention to this incident. John wants to emphasize the idea that from Christ's broken body there flowed the life-giving stream—water that the Spirit had given to believers in Jesus (7:38-39). Jesus said that if one drank this water, one would never thirst again (4:14).

The list of details that John includes and the other Gospels do not is long. A few of them have been mentioned here because they will help you interpret the Fourth Gospel. You may want to emphasize the theological concerns of the Fourth Gospel writer. John's purpose was primarily theological—that his readers would believe, would accept Jesus Christ, and would have eternal life in his name.

As did the other Gospel writers, John used the details he deemed most essential to his purpose. The whole Gospel story is the richer and more meaningful because each writer wrote according to his own purpose. Some group members may remember that Matthew, Mark, and Luke differ at other points with John. Point out to them that John had a different purpose in writing his Gospel. This difference shows up especially in the Passion narrative.

John 18:1-11. In a matter of hours, Jesus will die. How will he endure the indignities and pains of humiliation and death? The writer of John's Gospel is concerned with the events of the Passion narrative, and he wants us to think about their meaning. He would have us probe beneath the surface of events to grasp the import of what is really happening.

One example of the author's deeper purpose is the dramatic contrast he draws between Jesus' calm and serenity and Peter's tendency to panic in threatening situations. Jesus represents the stability and courage that come when one's relationship with God is rightly directed. Peter represents the confusion and uncertainty that come when one's relationship to God and life is misdirected. Peter has fine intentions, but he feels the pressures of a world heedless of God. He has been taught time and time again about the kingdom of God and the courage that comes when one is assured that the Kingdom is built on right relationships. Had Peter not listened to Jesus' parables? Did he not know the teachings of the Sermon on the Mount? But Peter, a courageous but impulsive disciple, was caught up in the fast-moving chain of events surrounding Jesus' passion (suffering) and death. He is like many modern viewers of television and other media who become accustomed to communicating in "sound bites" rather than taking time to reflect on what it means to live.

Peter needed, as we all need, the discipline that comes with meditation and prayer. These were Jesus' sources of courage.

John's Gospel draws a subtle contrast between the steady courage of Jesus and the unsteadiness of Peter. This contrast is apparent in the story of Jesus' arrest in the garden. When the troops come to arrest him, Jesus immediately goes out and asks, "Who is it you want?" The soldiers and police say, "Jesus of Nazareth." Quickly, Jesus says, "I am he." Jesus had thought prayerfully about his response in advance of the encounter he knew was coming. Jesus could have hidden in one of the many caves around the quiet and peaceful garden. Knowing that his hour had come, however, he went out bravely to meet his enemies.

When Peter sees what is happening, he acts with courage; but his is a foolhardy courage, a courage that has failed to say its prayers. Peter might have known his own actions would be rash and futile if he had observed Jesus closely enough.

A parable within this incident of Jesus' arrest applies to all of us. Jesus here demonstrates how the love of God meets the hostility and brutality of the world. Jesus bids us to meditate on the divine will and to pray. He sets an example for Peter and for us. In the upper room Jesus prayed for Peter and for us all. Peter fails, as we often fail, to heed Jesus' example in the critical situation in the garden.

In the garden, Jesus not only showed his bravery, he also demonstrated his authority. His was the authority of one who knew what he was about, whom he represented, and what his purpose was. We all know how important authority is. We see daily that this person exercises the authority of a parent, of a teacher, of a traffic control officer, of the city government, of a secretary of state. In a decent society all authority comes ultimately from God.

For this reason the armed group recoiled, and some men fell to the ground when Jesus appeared before them. They were awed, overwhelmed by the majesty of the lowly Galilean. Peter apparently missed the meaning of their actions.

After Peter had struck out blindly, Jesus calmly asked him, "Shall I not drink the cup the Father has given me?" In other words, "Let's remember my commitment to the divine will regardless of the dangers. God is present in what I am doing here."

Do we overlook the symbolism of the cup? Psalm 75:8 may shed light on Jesus' question to Peter:

> In the hand of the LORD is a cup
>> full of foaming wine mixed with spices;
> he pours it out, and all the wicked of the earth
>> drink it down to its very dregs.

In Jesus' mind, moreover, may have been the words of Psalm 116:13:

> I will lift up the cup of salvation
>> and call on the name of the LORD.

Certainly, Jesus was reminding Simon Peter that he came to lift the cup of salvation (suffering) for the sins of the world. The bitter cup Jesus has chosen and now agonizes over in the garden of Gethsemane represents his decision and his alone. He freely decides on his sacrificial death.

What is the cup of salvation? Why would John use this term to describe the decision of Jesus?

John 18:12-27. Jesus was brought first to Annas, the powerful and corrupt former high priest. Annas was a member of a priestly dynasty in Jerusalem. He had held the politicized office of high priest in AD 6–15. His five sons succeeded him. Then Caiaphas, his son-in-law, held the office, which under Roman rule had become a political plum to be bought and sold.

The high priest's office brought great wealth to the family, thanks to the influence and power that Annas, in conjunction with Caiaphas, wielded. Annas grew rich through abuses of the sacrificial system of the temple. His agents extorted money from the people by selling the sacrificial animals at outrageous prices. Outside the temple, a pair of doves cost a few pennies; inside the temple the agents of Annas could exact twenty times that amount for the same birds. Annas's agents acted like modern-day scalpers at athletic events. By managing shrewdly the system of traffic in sacred sacrifices, Annas and his family had amassed their wealth.

When Jesus drove the money changers from the temple, he placed himself in direct opposition to Annas's vested interests. In Annas's eyes Jesus became a marked man. Annas wanted to destroy Jesus because this prophet threatened his system of exploiting the people.

Annas was one in a long line of exploiters of religious feelings and loyalties for personal profit. How are religious groups sometimes exploited today? What is being done to insure more responsible financial accounting for money raised for charitable and religious causes? What can individuals do to see that their money does not go for too much in administrative costs and into the pockets of the unscrupulous or careless?

So Annas resolved to rid himself of an enemy who threatened to destroy his evil system. He resented Jesus' influence with the people. Annas ordered Jesus to be brought first to him. He set in motion the events that would lead to Jesus' death.

When Jesus appeared before Annas, Jesus' fate was already sealed. The hearing was brief, irregular, a sham, a violation of justice. Annas had already decided that Jesus should die. By failing to examine witnesses for Jesus, Annas violated the principles of Jewish justice (Deuteronomy 19:15). Jesus referred to this violation when he asked Annas why he didn't question some witnesses.

Annas sent Jesus on to Caiaphas. This leader in the Jewish religious hierarchy knew what was expected of him. He questioned Jesus briefly, took him to the Sanhedrin, and decided that Jesus was guilty of blasphemy. He knew the penalty of death by stoning was prescribed for this crime in the Jewish law. Caiaphas sent Jesus to Pilate.

A persisting theme in John's narrative is Simon Peter's reaction to the events of the trial. Peter presents us with a fascinating story. Three times he denies Jesus, and yet he stays close to Jesus during the court proceedings. (Only in John's Gospel is "another disciple" mentioned as being present; even then, other than gaining admittance for Peter, he is silent.)

You may want to discuss the character of Peter that is sketched in John 18. Peter is cowardly and brave, loyal and disloyal, stable and unstable.

Commentators generally seem to have been unfair to Peter, but his story is one repeated in some fashion by all of us. Peter did not live up to our Lord's expectations, but he always had another chance. We should remember that the battle was not over when the rooster crowed. We should remember Peter's final triumph through God's grace was his missionary work described in the Book of Acts and the key role he played in the spread of Christianity. When we are inclined to judge Peter too harshly, we should recall his sermon at Pentecost (Acts 2:14-36) and the important part he played in the formation of the church. The Roman Catholic Church has taught that Peter is the rock upon which the church is built. Protestants stress the belief that Peter's faith is the rock upon which the church is founded. Peter's faith is the work of God in human hearts. A church tradition teaches that Peter was crucified upside down because he felt it unworthy to be crucified in the same fashion as his Lord.

A man who had been reading the Bible commented to his pastor, "What rascals we find in the Bible!" His pastor replied, "True! What wonders God has wrought through these rascals!" Peter would look back on his career and admit that he was a rascal in some critical situations, but his life was a study in what the grace of God can do with a person's life. Christianity is the religion of new beginnings.

John 18:28-38a. The full account of the proceedings before Pilate will be covered in the next lesson. This passage presents to us some important questions raised in Jesus' first encounter with the Roman governor.

Why did the Jews in the company that arrested Jesus refuse to enter the palace of Pilate? What was the charge the Jewish leaders brought against Jesus? What was Pilate's interest in the controversy surrounding Jesus? What did Pilate want to see accomplished in the trial of Jesus? Why could the Jewish authorities not put Jesus to death?

Why does John stress the idea that Jesus would be "lifted up from the earth"? Read John 12:32. John wants to emphasize the way an unbelieving world would kill the Messiah. He wants to stress the necessity of the cross for the salvation of the world. Jesus must be exalted by this execution so that all people can see his sacrificial death.

What was Pilate's attitude toward the Jews? What was Jesus' offense? Why would Pilate be moved by Jesus' claim to be the Son of God and the Messiah?

In what sense is Jesus the king of the Jews? What is his purpose? What is the source of his power? Recall the conversation between Jesus and Pilate concerning Jesus' claim that he came to testify to the truth. Do you think Pilate would not stay for an answer? Why would Pilate be ill-equipped to discuss Jesus' claim? The central question for Pilate was, "What must I do with Jesus of Nazareth?" Do you agree that that is the main question facing each of us? Why or why not?

John 18:38b-40. Pilate gave the crowd the choice of Jesus or Barabbas. Why do you think the crowd wanted Jesus to be slain? What part do you think hatred played in their choice? John presents in the story of the trial the devastating results of hatred. What were these results? Insensitivity to the claims of our common humanity? a warping of our judgment? loss of a sense of balance? blindness to the reality of God's judgment? to God's forgiveness? to God's love?

DIMENSION THREE: WHAT DOES THE BIBLE MEAN TO ME?

Reflections on the Scripture

In Chapter 18, John confronts us with Jesus' calling of Peter to change. John does this by a subtle contrast between Jesus' calm command of the situation that goes before his death and Peter's nervous, hasty, and rash actions. Peter has many excellent qualities. He is sensitive, loyal, and brave. Peter remains to fight after all except "the other disciple" and himself have forsaken Jesus and fled. Yet Peter is quick-tempered, impulsive, weak in critical situations, and easily tempted to deny his loyalty to Jesus.

Peter had been called to the cause of Jesus many months before. He had responded eagerly; but now, long afterward, Jesus is still converting Peter. Salvation began with Jesus' call of Peter to greatness, though Peter hardly knew all this call meant. Peter was among those Christians who are being converted. God's work of conversion in him was continuing in every episode that involved the apostle as Jesus' death neared. So it is with us. Daily we are being converted. Daily we are summoned by Christ to choose his way and grow. The question put to Peter is ours also: "You are not one of his disciples, are you?"

So Peter's call is a call to greatness, as is ours. We are called to serve Christ in our families, in the church, in the community, and in the world—to bear witness to Christ whatever our vocation, whatever the situation we meet. That means lives of becoming—becoming our best selves. Peter's temptation and ours is ever to take the easy way out, to refuse to take a stand against the evil that crushes God's children. But we are called to value Christ's values, to love and serve those he loved and served.

We face daily the question posed by Pilate: Jesus or Barabbas?

We also face daily the prior question posed by Jesus. "Who is it you want?" The troops surrounding Jesus unwittingly phrased the answer to the question the whole world is asking, "Jesus of Nazareth."

We are called daily to celebrate Jesus' call to the Christian life and to grow.

Lead group members in a discussion of ways you and they think John 18 confronts us with the need to change. Do we see Peter's failings and mistakes in ourselves? What do we mean by saying we are daily being converted? What does it mean to be a disciple of Jesus today?

When he had received the drink, Jesus said, "It is finished." With that, he bowed his head and gave up his spirit (19:30).

11

CHRIST CRUCIFIED: "IT IS FINISHED"

John 19

DIMENSION ONE: WHAT DOES THE BIBLE SAY?

Answer these questions by reading John 19

1. What does Pilate do after the crowd cries out, "No, not him! Give us Barabbas!"? (19:1)

    He takes Jesus and has him flogged.

2. How do the soldiers treat Jesus? (19:2-3)

    They twist together a crown of thorns and put it on Jesus' head. They dress him in a purple robe, hail him as the king of the Jews, and slap him in the face.

3. What happens then? (19:4-6)

    Pilate goes out of his palace again and tells the crowd he is bringing Jesus out to them so that they will know he found no reason to accuse Jesus. When Jesus comes out, Pilate says to the crowd, "Here is the man!" But when the priests and the officials see Jesus, they cry out, "Crucify! Crucify!" Again Pilate tells Jesus' enemies to take Jesus and crucify him, for Pilate can "find no basis for a charge against him."

4. How do the Jewish leaders respond to this? (19:7)

    They say they have a law and by that law Jesus ought to die, because Jesus has "claimed to be the Son of God."

5. What is Pilate's response to this charge, and what does he do and say? (19:8-9a)

    He is afraid and enters the palace again to ask Jesus a question, "Where do you come from?"

6. How does Jesus answer Pilate? (19:9b)

   Jesus does not reply to Pilate's question.

7. What does Pilate now say, and what does Jesus reply? (19:10-11)

   Pilate asks Jesus if he does not know Pilate has the power to release or to crucify him. Jesus says, "You would have no power over me if it were not given to you from above." Jesus says that those who have handed him over to Pilate's hands have the greater sin.

8. What does Pilate seek to do then, and what do the Jewish leaders say to this? (19:12)

   Pilate tries to set Jesus free, but the Jews keep shouting, "If you let this man go, you are no friend of Caesar."

9. What does Pilate do when he hears these words? (19:13-14)

   He brings Jesus out, and Pilate "sat down on the judge's seat." He says to the Jews, "Here is your king."

10. What do the Jewish leaders say to this? (19:15)

    They cry out, "Take him away! Take him away! Crucify him!"

11. What does Pilate do then? (19:16)

    Pilate hands Jesus over to the Jewish leaders to be crucified.

12. Where do the soldiers take Jesus for crucifixion? (19:17)

    The soldiers take Jesus to "the place of the Skull (which in Aramaic is called Golgotha)" to crucify him.

13. When they crucify Jesus, what does Pilate write for a title to be put on the cross? How do the chief priests of the Jews respond to the title? (19:19-21)

   Pilate writes in three languages—Aramaic, Latin, and Greek—the title "JESUS OF NAZARETH, THE KING OF THE JEWS." The chief priests of the Jews object, claiming the title should read, "This man claimed to be king of the Jews."

14. What do the soldiers do that fulfills the Scripture? (19:23-24)

    They divide Jesus' clothes into four shares and decide by lot who will get the seamless garment.

15. What does Jesus say from the cross to his mother and to the beloved disciple? (19:25-27)

    Jesus says to his mother, "Woman, here is your son." To the disciple Jesus says, "Here is your mother."

16. What are Jesus' next words from the cross, and what do the soldiers give him? (19:28-30)

    Jesus says, "I am thirsty," and the soldiers press to his mouth a sponge of wine vinegar fixed on a stalk of hyssop. After receiving the vinegar, Jesus says, "It is finished."

17. Who asks Pilate for the body of Jesus for burial? (19:38)

    Joseph of Arimathea, a disciple of Jesus in secret because of fear of the Jewish leaders, asks Pilate for Jesus' body.

18. How does Nicodemus figure in the burial of Jesus? (19:39)

    He brings to the tomb a mixture of myrrh and aloes, "about seventy-five pounds," for Jesus' burial.

19. When and where is Jesus buried? (19:41-42)

    On the Jewish day of Preparation, Jesus is buried near the place where he was crucified, in a tomb in a garden "in which no one had ever been laid."

DIMENSION TWO:
WHAT DOES THE BIBLE MEAN?

Introduction. The dramatic encounter between Jesus and Pilate that began in Chapter 18 continues in Chapter 19. The story of the conflict reads something like a Greek tragedy, but it ends with Jesus' words of victory on the cross, "It is finished." Pilate's great dilemma—his tragic destiny—is expressed in the question: What shall I do with Jesus of Nazareth?

Jesus is sentenced to a criminal's death by the Roman ruler and goes to Golgotha, where he is crucified between two others. John tells the story of Jesus on the cross with short, powerful strokes. The soldiers gamble for Jesus' clothes; Jesus asks the beloved disciple to care for his

GENESIS to REVELATION **JOHN**

mother and John then takes Mary into his own home. Jesus climaxes the drama with the words "I thirst" and "It is finished." Then he bows his head and yields to death. He who has lifted for all humankind the cup of salvation goes out with the taste of sour wine on his lips.

The Jewish leaders ask Pilate to have the legs of the crucified men broken and their bodies removed before the beginning of the sabbath. When the soldiers come to Jesus, they find he is already dead. The rapidly approaching start of the sabbath necessitated hurrying along the process, so that Jesus' body could be handled without violating the proscription against work on the sabbath. Breaking the legs of the crucified men would force even more weight on their diaphragms. The greater pressure would reduce their breathing ability and hasten death.

Jesus' followers take his body away and bury it near the Crucifixion site in a garden—in a tomb where no one has ever been laid.

The calm of John's description of the burial contrasts sharply with the explosive fury of the crowd and Pilate's turmoil as he wrestles with his decision.

John will continue the story. In the quiet we shall await the Resurrection.

John 19:1-16. Pilate was procurator, governor, of Palestine from AD 26 to 35. Pilate had been appointed by Augustus Caesar to a post that was troubled by many problems. Resenting Roman rule, the Jewish people constantly threatened rebellion. We know little about Pilate's background; but we may assume he was a strong, successful administrator. A hard assignment like governing the area of Palestine would be reserved for a shrewd and able politician.

On going to his post, Pilate made a number of mistakes that turned the Jews against him. For example, he showed his contempt for their religion by refusing to remove the image of Caesar from his standard when he entered Jerusalem with his troops. Former governors had deferred to the religious feelings of the Jews by removing the metal image of Caesar from their standards. This image was official recognition that the emperor was a god.

Deploring the insensitivity of Pilate, the Jewish leaders begged him repeatedly to remove the graven image, but he refused to be swayed by what he regarded as Jewish superstition. The Jews persisted in their requests until the crafty ruler met with them in his amphitheater to discuss his insult to their faith. Pilate brought in his soldiers and told the Jews that if they did not drop their requests, he would kill them all on the spot. Baring their necks, the Jews defied Pilate, daring the armed men to carry out Pilate's order.

Pilate did not want to cut down defenseless people, so he backed down and agreed to remove the image from his standard.

In another incident Pilate raided the temple treasury in order to get money for building a much-needed aqueduct for supplying Jerusalem with water. Pilate's actions set off rioting in the streets. The governor sent his soldiers, dressed in plain clothing and carrying concealed weapons, to mix with the crowds. At a given signal, the soldiers attacked the mob and clubbed and stabbed many Jews to death. The enraged populace threatened to retaliate against Pilate by demanding that the emperor remove the governor from office.

So when Pilate dealt with the Jews concerning what to do with Jesus, both sides had grievances. Behind the events of Jesus' trial stood a history of conflict and maneuvering for power. Many Jews were determined to "get Pilate" for what he had done to them and to their religion. The Jews had once before reported Pilate's injustices to Rome, and Pilate did not want them to do this again. He wanted to give the impression in Rome that he was master of the situation in Palestine. But his past actions came now to haunt him. Pilate knew the Jewish leaders could subject him to blackmail if he handled the trial of Jesus in a way that would displease them.

Most scholars, however, think Pilate did not want to send Jesus to his death. He wanted to compromise the issue so that Jesus would be punished enough to satisfy the Jewish leaders; but Pilate misjudged, at first at least, their hatred and intentions.

What did Pilate do with Jesus? First, he tried to get the Jewish leaders to take on his [Pilate's] responsibility. God was confronting Pilate in the man Jesus of Nazareth, and no human being could take on Pilate's responsibility for an answer to the question God raised. Every person must make his or her own decision concerning Jesus Christ, and it is the most important decision of one's life. Pilate had Jesus flogged (brutally whipped) with the idea that this torture would cause the Jews to take pity on Jesus. His effort failed.

Pilate was a poor judge of ways to get along with the Jews. He expressed contempt for them and refused to be involved in Jewish disputes. He sensed in Jesus a splendor that fascinated him through all the controversy. He wanted to release Jesus, but he feared the Jews. He was curious about Jesus; so he was prompted to ask ultimate questions like Where are you from? and What is truth? Pilate may have sensed that Jesus was from God and that ultimate truth was being laid before him and his foes by the man of Galilee.

Pilate presided over the strangest trial of history. But he, not Jesus, was really on trial. Jesus was calm and straightforward in his testimony, but his kingdom was not this world of broken faith and moral and social corruption. Jesus came to bear witness to the truth—to live the truth before our eyes—to be the truth as the culminating revelation of God. Jesus was often silent, but his silence spoke the language of eternal life.

John 19:17-22. Pilate's defeat at the trial of Jesus is announced in the simple words of John 19:16: "Finally Pilate handed him over to them to be crucified." This was Pilate's confession that he was too cowardly to stand against the Jews. The governor delivered Jesus to the Roman soldiers for execution. The soldiers followed the usual method of crucifixion (see the participant book, pages 99–100). They led Jesus out to the place of the Skull, a gaunt hill that likely got its name from its resemblance to a human skull.

John does not tell us that on the way to the Crucifixion Jesus found the cross too heavy to bear and that Simon of Cyrene was required to carry it for him (Mark 15:21). John stresses the idea that Jesus bears his cross for the redemption of the world, but we also are to take up our crosses and to follow him. We are not to call trivial inconveniences and irritations our crosses; our crosses can only be laid on us by Christ. These are accepted willingly, for we are to be Jesus' witnesses in the world. Christians die with Jesus Christ and rise with him to a transformed life.

The Gospel of John does not describe the dreadful details of the Crucifixion. He is more interested in the cosmic drama being enacted on the cross. Many of the hymns of the church capture the pathos of that event. Invite group members to look through the Passion hymns in your church's hymnal. How is the cross characterized? Many images come to mind: the "wondrous cross," "shameful tree," "faithful cross, sign of triumph," "noblest tree." The poets' words remind us of a need to see the cross in this broad, universal context that has profound meaning for each of us. Something world-shaking is going on here.

Over the cross, Pilate wrote, "JESUS OF NAZARETH, THE KING OF THE JEWS." These words were written in Aramaic, in Latin, and in Greek, three great languages of the ancient world, languages that have entered a thousand tongues of our world to proclaim the universal King and Savior. Pilate refused to change the words. They represent the record of his life and our own: "What I have written, I have written."

John 19:23-37. What are people doing while Jesus is on the cross? John gives us a vivid picture of some of the people who were nearby and witnessed the Crucifixion.

John pictures for us the soldiers gambling for Jesus' clothing. Here John symbolizes the world's indifference to Jesus' mission and death. Jesus came to tell people something by demonstrating the love of God in human life. But the soldiers, like many others, were engaged in a trivial pursuit in the midst of tragic events.

The indifference of the soldiers is like the indifference of many Christians during the Holocaust when Jews by the millions were sent to the gas chambers. The American folk hymn "Were You There" may be recalled by Christians to pierce the hard shell of our complacency over the evils that beset our nation.

Were you there when they crucified my Lord? . . .

Sometimes it causes me to tremble, tremble, tremble.

The words should startle us awake. Are we still stirred by the sacrifice of Jesus for our salvation? Do the lines of the hymn cause us to probe whether we may be indifferent when Jesus is bidding us from the cross to involve ourselves in the world's agonies?

Contrast the indifference shown by the soldiers with the response of the beloved disciple when Jesus says to him, "Here is your mother." The Gospel tells us that from that time John took Mary into his own home to care for her. Literally one with the world on his shoulders, Jesus sees his mother and entrusts her care to the faithful disciple who stands near the cross. Here Jesus bids us remember that there is no conflict between our duty to the community (whether local or worldwide) and our duty to parents. In the hour of his death, Jesus repeats the lesson his whole life has taught—he suffers our real human woes. On the cross, he knows the pain of thirst.

John presents Jesus' answer to the religions and philosophies that were current in the early centuries of Christianity—systems that argued that spirit was wholly good and matter was wholly evil. This way of thinking was called *gnosticism*. It taught that God never would share in the contamination of the flesh that the Incarnation would involve. Matter is evil, the gnostics insisted. Gnosticism denied the Incarnation and the Prologue to the Gospel of John when it says, "The Word became flesh." Gnostics argued that Jesus did not have a real body that suffered the pains of the flesh. Jesus was understood as a pure spirit, and the gnostic religions were purely "spiritual" religions.

On the cross, Jesus refuted the gnostics' teachings of detachment from the world of matter. God has made human beings with body, mind, and spirit; and we are called to serve him in the marketplace and wherever else our duties take us.

"It is finished"—these were Jesus' last words on the cross. The mission he had been sent to accomplish was now completed. Jesus of Nazareth—he is our best proof of God. So the cry "It is finished" was a shout of victory that would be made plainer to the disciples on the morning of the Resurrection.

John continues his account of the "Word made flesh" with the act of the soldier in piercing Jesus' side with the spear. From Jesus' side there flowed blood and water. It was a strange phenomenon, a sign that attested to the reality that Jesus was a real man and had a real body. This event was another way of disproving the gnostics' belief that Jesus was not fully human.

John sees in the incident of the issuing of blood and water from Jesus' side a symbol of two church sacraments. One sacrament is based on water—namely, baptism. The other is based on blood; it is Holy Communion. In baptism the water is a sign of God's cleansing and healing mercy. In the fruit of the vine of the sacrament we have the sign of the cleansing blood of Jesus' sacrifice. The cross, therefore, speaks to us of the supreme love of God.

In his *Imitation of Christ*, Thomas à Kempis presents to us a summary of what the cross may mean for us:

- In the Cross is salvation, in the Cross is life, in the Cross is protection against our enemies, in the Cross is infusion of heavenly sweetness, in the Cross is strength of mind, in the Cross joy of spirit, in the Cross the height of virtue, in the Cross the perfection of holiness. There is no salvation of the soul, nor hope of everlasting life, but in the Cross. Take up therefore thy Cross and follow Jesus, and thou shalt go into life everlasting. He went before, bearing His Cross, and died for thee on the Cross; that thou also mayest bear thy Cross and desire to die on the Cross. For if thou be dead with Him, thou shalt also in like manner live with Him. And if thou share His punishment, thou shalt also share His glory.
- Behold! in the Cross all doth consist, and in our dying thereon all lieth; for there is no other way unto life, and unto true inward peace, but the way of the holy Cross, and of daily mortification. Walk where thou wilt, seek whatsoever thou wilt, thou shalt not find a higher way above, nor a safer way below, than the way of the holy Cross.[1]

John 19:38-42. After the death of Jesus, two members of the Sanhedrin came forward to arrange for his burial. Joseph of Arimathea, who was a secret disciple of Jesus because of fear of the Jews, went to Pilate and asked for the Lord's body. Then Nicodemus, also a secret disciple of Jesus, brought to the tomb sweet spices for the Lord's burial.

Both disciples held responsible positions in the Jewish power structure. Both risked disgrace and loss of influence if they became known as followers of Jesus. Both, however, suppressed their fears and paid tribute to the lowly Galilean.

Jesus taught that when he was lifted up, he would draw all human beings to himself. His cross drew these two members of the Sanhedrin to him. The cross made heroes of both men. So they buried Jesus in a new grave in the garden, in a tomb in which no one had ever been laid.

DIMENSION THREE:
WHAT DOES THE BIBLE MEAN TO ME?

What Shall We Do With Jesus?

Lead the class members in a discussion and meditation on the section in the participant book entitled "What Shall We Do With Jesus?"

What mistakes did Pilate make that set the Jews against him before Jesus was brought to trial? How did Pilate try to evade responsibility for his decision concerning Jesus? Why may Christians conclude that Pilate lost the battle over Jesus?

In what ways do we evade making decisions about Jesus? How often in the past week have you spoken up for your faith? How often in the past week have you avoided taking a stand on an issue that would have identified you as a follower of Jesus?

Why can we say that Pilate wanted to be his own God? How do modern people show this same desire? Do we also desire to manipulate others, to wield power, and to be our God?

Read the definitions of a Christian in Dimension Three of the participant book. What do you think is Christ's vision of the kingdom of God? Do we share it? What evidence do we put forth that we want what Christ wants? Do we, like Pilate, seek ways out of our responsibility? How?

Do you agree that Pilate was defeated in the encounter over whether Jesus should go to the cross? Why or why not? What do you think cross-bearing means in the Christian faith? What does it mean for Christians to die with Christ? Is this death always a physical dying? Is it, perhaps, harder to live for Christ than to die for him? Why or why not? Why do you think John does not describe the Crucifixion in detail?

What were the good and bad qualities in Pilate? What kind of record did Pilate write? What kind are we writing?

Why do you think Joseph and Nicodemus were willing to risk their prestige and fine community standing to bury Jesus' body? Why was the cross Jesus' supreme act of courage? How do you think this act affected Joseph and Nicodemus? How do you think Jesus' death on the cross can affect each of us?

---

[1] From *The Imitation of Christ*, revised translation, by Thomas à Kempis (Grosset and Dunlap, 1935), page 109.

Again Jesus said, "Peace be with you! As the Father has sent me, I am sending you" (20:21).

12

CHRIST IS RISEN!
John 20

DIMENSION ONE:
WHAT DOES THE BIBLE SAY?

Answer these questions by reading John 20

1. When does Mary Magdalene come to the tomb early and see the stone had been removed from the entrance? (20:1)

Mary comes "early on the first day of the week, while it was still dark."

2. When Mary runs from the tomb, whom does she meet? (20:2)

Mary meets Simon Peter and the other disciple, "the one Jesus loved."

3. What does Mary say to them? (20:2)

She tells them, "They have taken the Lord out of the tomb, and we don't know where they have put him!"

4. Who outruns Peter to be the first disciple to reach the tomb? (20:4)

The other disciple outruns Peter.

5. What do the other disciple and Peter see on reaching the tomb? (20:6-7)

They see the strips of linen and the burial cloth that had been around Jesus' head.

6. What do the two disciples do? (20:8)

They both enter the tomb. The "other disciple . . . saw and believed."

7. What does Mary do and see? (20:11-12)

She stands outside the tomb crying, bends over to look into the tomb, and sees two angels in white sitting where Jesus' body had been.

8. What do the angels ask Mary, and what is Mary's reply? (20:13)

They ask Mary why she is crying. She replies that she cries because Jesus has been taken away and she does not know where they have put him.

9. Whom does Mary now see, and what does he tell her? (20:14-17)

She sees Jesus, but mistakes him for the gardener. Jesus calls Mary's name and tells her not to hold him for he has not yet ascended to the Father. He tells her to go to his brothers and to tell them that he is returning to his God and theirs.

10. What is Mary's message to the disciples? (20:18)

Her message is that she has seen the Lord. Then she delivers the message Jesus gave her for them.

11. What happens on the evening of the first day? (20:19-21)

Jesus comes to the disciples who are behind locked doors. He greets them with the words, "Peace be with you!" and shows them his hands and his side. He says to them again, "Peace be with you! As the Father has sent me, I am sending you."

12. What is the response of the disciples to all this? (20:20b)

The disciples are overjoyed.

13. What does Jesus do and say next? (20:22-23)

He breathes on the disciples and tells them to receive the Holy Spirit. He says if they forgive the sins of anyone, these persons would be forgiven; that if they do not forgive the sins of any they are not forgiven.

14. What do the disciples tell Thomas when he arrives? (20:25a)

They tell him that they had seen the Lord.

15. What is Thomas's reply? (20:25b)

He says he must see the mark of the nails and put his finger in their mark and also place his hand in Jesus' side before he will believe.

16. What happens a week later? (20:26-27)

Jesus comes among the disciples again. He told Thomas to touch him, to stop doubting, and to believe.

17. What is Thomas's response? (20:28)

He answers, "My Lord and my God!"

18. What does Jesus say? (20:29)

Jesus says that Thomas believes because he has seen, but that those who believe without seeing are blessed.

19. What was John's purpose in writing the Gospel? (20:31)

It was written so that "you may believe that Jesus is the Messiah, the Son of God, and that by believing you may have life in his name."

DIMENSION TWO: WHAT DOES THE BIBLE MEAN?

John 20:1-10. Mary Magdalene, the much forgiven sinner, came to the tomb first on Easter Day. Mary came early. As John's Gospel says, she came while it was "still dark."

The Fourth Evangelist does not mention the "other women" who were with Mary, but he implies their presence in the words, "They have taken the Lord out of the tomb, and we don't know where they have put him!" We turn to the Synoptics (Matthew, Mark, and Luke) for the information that with Mary Magdalene were Mary, the mother of James the younger, and Salome (Mark 15:40; Matthew 27:56) or Mary, the mother of James and Joanna (Luke 24:10).

In the early morning light Mary Magdalene was able to see that the stone has been taken from the entrance of the tomb. She ran to share this news with others, and she met Peter and the other disciple. She told them the tomb was empty. Mary announced a reality that she did not comprehend: the faith of Jesus is the faith of the empty tomb. This is the message the church must proclaim today. Christians worship not a grave but the living Lord. Jesus' body has been raised from death, so that he is present everywhere.

In the Fourth Evangelist's view, the material body of Jesus has been changed into a spiritual body. We do not understand all that this means, but Christians believe that our unique personalities are raised in the Resurrection. Flesh and blood, the bodies we now have, will not inherit life eternal; but in the mystery of God's grace we shall be given the spiritual bodies we need to live in the presence of him who dwells in eternal light.

Peter and the other disciple beheld a symbol of this reality when they saw the burial cloths of Jesus. The cloths were neatly folded and put away as a person who irons allows no wrinkle or disarray to mar his or her work. If thieves had come to steal Jesus' body, they would have taken him in his burial cloths. They would have left signs of haste.

The attentions of Peter and the beloved disciple were therefore centered on the neatly folded burial cloths and their meaning. Peter saw the cloths, but John was the first to see and believe. The beloved disciple was in a better position to believe in the Christ because he had great love for the Messiah. John saw and believed that Jesus had risen from the dead.

Countless Christians since the time of Mary Magdalene and the beloved disciple have also seen and believed. They have been convinced by what Christ has done in their lives. At Eastertide we sing the words of "Christ Jesus Lay in Death's Strong Bands" by Martin Luther:

> Christ Jesus lay in death's strong bands,
>   for our offenses given;
> but now at God's right hand he stands,
>   and brings us life from heaven;
> wherefore let us joyful be,
>   and sing to God right thankfully
> loud songs of Alleluia!
> Alleluia!
>
> It was a strange and dreadful strife
>   when life and death contended;
> the victory remained with life;
>   the reign of death was ended.
> Stripped of power, no more it reigns,
>   an empty form alone remains;
> death's sting is lost forever!
> Alleluia!

John 20:11-18. Mary's Lord had been crucified between two thieves—"numbered with the transgressors" (Isaiah 53:12; Luke 22:37). As she cried Mary peeped into the tomb. Unlike Peter and John, she did not notice the burial cloths. Her eyes fixed on two angels in white, one sitting by the head and the other sitting by the feet where the body of Jesus had lain. By including the presence of the angels John wanted to emphasize that God was present in the events of the empty tomb. God was there to speak to the sorrow of Mary.

When the angels asked why Mary was weeping she said, "They have taken my Lord away, . . . and I don't know where they have put him." Mary wanted to "take him away," perhaps to give Jesus' body an honored burial, not realizing that Joseph and Nicodemus had already prepared the body (John 19:38-42). When Jesus first spoke to Mary, she did not recognize his voice. Mistaking him for the gardener, she asked Jesus to tell her where the body lay so she could go find it and give it a proper burial.

Then Jesus spoke Mary's name, causing her to turn around and face him. Mary had an experience that is similar to our own. We know how we are affected when we hear our name called. Modern salespeople are taught that there is power in the calling of a person's name. The hearing of one's name shakes up the person and involves him or her in what is going on.

Mary was looking for Jesus among the dead, not looking for him as the living Savior. How many of us look for Christ among the tombs? We search the historic reports of his presence long ago, and that is well. We are ready to believe these accounts. But as record and history these reports do not touch us. A living Christ—one who confronts us at the office, in the home, in the school, in the business and political systems—that One puts us under obligation. Mary did not find Christ; for Christ found Mary, just as he finds us.

Our God is the God who seeks us. God pursues us unceasingly. When John wrote his Gospel, he was continuing the theme of God's search for the human being that we have chronicled in writings of the Pentateuch, the prophets, and the Wisdom Literature. The high points of the Old Testament come in the expressions of the love of God for Israel—as in Jeremiah 31:3: "I have loved you with an everlasting love; / I have drawn you with unfailing kindness." The God who pursues us emerges most clearly in Psalm 139. (Read to group members the first twelve verses of this psalm.)

Mary sought Christ in the graveyard; but she did not recognize him when he appeared to her, just as we do not always recognize him. He did not come to her in the expected way. He came in no thunderstorms or public fanfares. In her mixed disappointment and hope, Christ came to Mary tenderly.

So it is that in times of sorrow and loss, when everything seems to have collapsed for us, we may know that God's love does not fail us. That is the meaning of the Resurrection.

When Mary recognized Jesus, she tried to hold him, but he dissuaded her. Jesus, in effect, told Mary not to hold on to him in the flesh with its limitations. Instead, she should cling to him through his reunion with God after the Ascension, which would be Jesus' last appearance on earth.

John 20:19-23. What are this individual's credentials? This question is often asked in our society. Candidates for political office and high court appointments are required to answer it.

Physicians put their diplomas up on their walls. Teachers, mechanics, computer technicians, and nurses are required to furnish credentials. Young graduates of educational institutions are carefully coached on how to prepare résumés of their scholastic and work experiences so that prospective employers will be favorably impressed and will employ them. Writers, soldiers, and scientists earn their credentials by their performances. Feodor Dostoevski, the greatest of Russian novelists, was once taunted by a critic who demanded to know by what right he could speak for the Russian people. He simply pulled up his trouser cuffs and revealed the scars of Siberian chains.

What were Jesus' credentials? On Easter evening he came into the presence of his disciples and said to them, "Peace be with you!" Then he showed them his hands and his side that bore the wounds of the Crucifixion. The cross was his crown of glory, the sign by which he would be known throughout the world.

Jesus was preparing his disciples, a defeated and discouraged lot, to begin a ministry that would ultimately win the world to him. In the aftermath of the cross he brought courage to these disciples. The cross was once a symbol of humiliation and disgrace. Now it was the symbol of joy and victory.

Jesus' mission has been accomplished. His credentials will forever be the cross. He has been raised from the dead, thus conquering the two worst enemies of humankind: sin and death.

What does he do now? Jesus gives to the disciples the Holy Spirit, breathing on them to symbolize the giving of himself—the giving of new life. The Spirit would give power, imagination, and zeal to the disciples and the church.

Jesus gives this same Spirit to us, the same Spirit who works in every human situation, bringing good out of evil. Without the Holy Spirit, we can do nothing. With the Spirit, the church can preach the forgiveness of sins to the whole world and mediate the love of God to all people.

In the encounter with the disciples, then, Jesus gives us the selfsame message he gave to his first disciples: "As the Father has sent me, I am sending you." John's Gospel is a missionary book. It tells us and all humankind that love will triumph in the whole world because Christ is risen.

John 20:24-29. We have met Thomas in the study of 11:16 and 14:5. In the first passage Thomas, called Didymus (the Twin), challenges his fellow disciples to go with Jesus to Bethany where they could all die together. Thomas was willing to be a martyr for Jesus. In the second passage Thomas voices the skeptical statement, "Lord, we don't know where you are going, so how can we know the way?" Jesus replies, "I am the way and the truth and the life. No one comes to the Father, except through me."

Thomas knew the claim of Jesus that Jesus and the Father are one. He understood the consequences of being a disciple of Jesus. In the first verse cited about him, Thomas was courageous; but he was weak later when with the other disciples he forsook Jesus and fled.

After the Crucifixion, Thomas took time to think matters over. He wanted to see what would happen next. We might apply to Thomas the characterization that Charles Dickens gave of Joe Gargery: "He was a mild, good-natured, sweet-tempered, easy-going, foolish, dear fellow—a sort of Hercules in strength and also in weakness."[1] This description might be applied to many of us.

The disciples told Thomas the Lord had risen from the dead. For Thomas this claim was just too much. He would not believe the disciples' report until he could see for himself.

When Jesus came into the room where Thomas was, he challenged Thomas to examine his credentials: the wounds of the Crucifixion. These were the marks of Jesus' success! Thomas asked for tangible proof of the Resurrection. Jesus gave him proof of the Crucifixion. Jesus' presence was all the proof the disciple needed of the Resurrection. We prove our Lord by the encounter with him—by experience. This truth grasped Thomas and caused him to exclaim: "My Lord and my God!"

John 20:30-31. John wrote his work to win us to the belief that Jesus is the Christ, the Anointed One, the Son of God, and that believing in him we may have life in his name. John tells us of the God who demonstrates his love and care for us individually and for the world.

This story may help us in our meditations on that love and care:

A woman was driving alone through a very large American city. The traffic was congested and noisy—bumper-to-bumper at times—so that the woman became utterly confused. Having made three false turns, she lost the way. She finally managed to stop at a service station where she could ask for travel information. The woman got out of her car, went inside the station, and explained her predicament to an employee.

The service station attendant got down a map of the city, saying, "So you're lost. I don't know how you'll ever get to the interstate. There is much street construction along the way, and all the signs have been changed." The attendant scratched his head, pored over the map, and said, "You'll have to go back the way you came and take the right turns."

Said the woman, "I could never do that. I don't know how I got here in the first place."

Said the attendant: "You'll need to go southeast through the city. Let's see, you take a right on the boulevard, go past four traffic lights, turn left at the top of the hill, cross three traffic lights, and turn left at the river bridge. . . . No, that won't do. You'll run into road construction. Everything's torn up for six blocks. You can't get there from here."

After half an hour of the attendant's perplexity, another woman who had heard it all stepped forward and said to the other woman, "I'll show you the way. I'll lead you there. Just follow close to me. I'll drive slowly so the cars can't cut in between us."

The second woman put her small daughter in her car. Then she drove many miles through tortuous traffic, making many turns. Finally, she stopped her car at the entrance to the cloverleaf, got out, and walked back to give instructions about where to exit on the interstate. She laughed, wished the other woman well, and waved goodbye.

Here we have a parable of the journey of faith. Jesus came to show us the way and to help us reach our human destination.

DIMENSION THREE:
WHAT DOES THE BIBLE MEAN TO ME?

The class members may discuss the following questions or use the meditation in the participant book.

Searching for Jesus

Use the story above to begin discussing the path you have had to take to feel as if you have found Jesus Christ or an answer to a spiritual question you have. Include the tools and methods, including the Bible, you used to better see your path.

Do we sometimes fail to recognize the Savior's voice when he speaks to us? How does Christ speak to us? How should we listen for his voice?

Christ is risen. So what? What does the Resurrection mean to us in these modern times? What did the Resurrection mean to Mary Magdalene? to Peter? to John? to Thomas? to other early Christians?

How are we like Thomas? Do we, like he did, wait for conclusive proof for our faith? Do we search for a firsthand religious experience that touches our minds as well as our hearts? What can Thomas's experience teach us about our faith?

---

[1] From *Great Expectations*, by Charles Dickens (Holt, Rhinehart and Winston, 1967), page 6.

Jesus did many other things as well. If every one of them were written down, I suppose that even the whole world would not have room for the books that would be written (21:25).

13

VICTORY AND CHRIST'S CALL

John 21

DIMENSION ONE: WHAT DOES THE BIBLE SAY?

Answer these questions by reading John 21

1. To whom does Jesus reveal himself by the Sea of Galilee? (21:1-2)

   He reveals himself to these disciples: Simon Peter, Thomas, Nathanael, the sons of Zebedee, and two other disciples.

2. What does Simon Peter say he is going to do, and what happens? (21:3)

   Peter says he is going fishing. Others join him; and they fish all night, catching nothing.

3. Who is standing on the shore early the next morning? (21:4)

   Jesus is standing on the shore, but the disciples do not recognize him.

4. When he asks the disciples if they had caught any fish and receives a negative reply, what does Jesus tell them to do? (21:5-6a)

   He tells the disciples to cast their net on the right side of the boat, "and you will find some [fish]."

5. What do the disciples do then, and what results from their action? (21:6b)

   They cast their net where Jesus had told them to. They are unable to haul in the large number of fish.

6. Who first recognizes Jesus, and what does he say? (21:7a)

   The "disciple whom Jesus loved" recognizes Jesus and says, "It is the Lord!"

7. What does Peter do when he hears this? (21:7b)
    He put on his clothes and "jumped into the water."

8. What do the other disciples do? (21:8)
    They bring in the boat, "towing the net full of fish."

9. What do the disciples see when they get to land, and what does Jesus say to them? (21:9-10)
    They see a charcoal fire "with fish on it, and some bread." Jesus says, "Bring some of the fish you have just caught."

10. What does Peter do then, and what does Jesus say to the disciples? (21:11-12)
    "Peter climbed back into the boat and dragged the net ashore." Jesus tells the disciples to come to breakfast.

11. What is said after they finish breakfast? (21:15-19)
    Jesus asks Peter three times if the disciple loves him. Peter replies three times that he loves Jesus. Each time Jesus tells Peter to care for his sheep. Jesus, suggesting the death by which Peter would die, says to Peter, "Follow me!"

DIMENSION TWO:
WHAT DOES THE BIBLE MEAN?

The Epilogue. Many scholars maintain that John 21 is an appendix written by a different person than the one who wrote Chapters 1–20. They have strong reasons for questioning the conclusion that John the apostle (who is identified as the beloved disciple) wrote the final chapter. Detailed and comprehensive studies of the language and literary construction of the chapter lie behind their questioning. We do not know who wrote Chapter 21, but it is possible to suppose that a person who had been closely related to the apostolic author wrote it.

The questions of authorship, however, are secondary questions; for we should not let the problems of authorship take precedence over the primary question: Is the chapter true? The overwhelming evidence is that it is.

What is the concern of the author of Chapter 21? One purpose of the author was to remind the church that Peter, who had betrayed Jesus, had been forgiven and restored to his old status as natural leader of the apostles. The author also wanted to combat the false idea that Christ would come before the death of John, the last of the apostles.

Many scholars think the author of Chapter 21 also wrote to affirm the reality of the Resurrection. The risen Christ was no mere phantom, no mere vision cherished by the confused disciples. He was no hallucination, but a person of flesh and blood who had been raised from the tomb. Jesus indeed walked in the world and cooked and ate fish.

Chapter 21 indicates that a pure spirit probably would not concern itself with telling fishermen where the fishing would be best for a fine catch. A pure spirit would not build a fire by the sea and cook a meal to feed hungry fishermen.

Chapter 21, then, is in full harmony with the whole message of the Gospel. The Epilogue agrees with the Prologue: "The Word became flesh and made his dwelling among us." John's Gospel will never let us forget this reality. The characters of his drama get mixed up in the material world.

John 21:1-14. This section of Scripture is in accord with John's Gospel in the way it symbolizes truth. One example is indicated by the report that 153 fish were caught by the disciples. The writer does not describe the catch as a miracle or as a "sign," but he is concerned to bring concrete detail into his narrative; he wants to tell us the catch was a huge one and that Jesus knew where the fish could be caught. The writer wants us to see that the report of the catch has a deeper meaning.

Scholars have made many attempts to unravel John's hidden meaning regarding the catch of fish. Jerome has given us perhaps the best explanation. In an allegorical fashion Jerome declares that there were 153 different kinds of fish in the sea. The catch includes every kind of fish, and the number symbolizes the reality that in the future all nations will be gathered to Jesus Christ.

William Barclay has said that the whole catch of fish was placed in the net, and the net was not broken by the weight of the fish. The net symbolizes the church, and the church has room for persons of all nations. Again we have the clear note of universality affirmed in the Gospel. The Christian gospel excludes no one because of color, class, or nationality: and "the embrace of the Church," says Barclay, "is as universal as the love of God in Jesus Christ."[1]

At the heart of the Fourth Gospel is its author's resolve to show that in Jesus Christ we have the real Incarnation and the fulfillment of all human hopes. This is why Chapter 21 continues to combat the idea that Jesus Christ seemed to be something that he was not.

John took issue with the docetists, a heretical group of religionists who believed that Jesus Christ had no fleshly existence but came to earth in a human "semblance" without being corrupted by contact with the flesh and with the material existence. The docetists were part of the mixed and diverse system of thinkers, ideas, and writings that became known as gnosticism. The gnostics (from the Greek word *gnosis*, meaning knowledge) claimed that they possessed a knowledge that freed them from the fragmentary, the illusory, and the evil world. They said a rift existed between appearance and reality. Believing the fleshly existence was evil, they sought to shun it.

Gnosticism plagued the church for the first four centuries of its history; its downfall came with the work of Athanasius and other theologians who championed the faith that "God was reconciling the world to himself in Christ" (2 Corinthians 5:19) and that Christ was fully human and fully divine.

Gnostic ideas and attitudes have persisted in the modern church, however, and their persistence is what Amos N. Wilder calls the "false spirituality" of the church. Give some time to elaborate on evidences of this "false spirituality" in the church today. (See the participant book, pages 114–116.)

What methods of escape from the pain and struggle of the world do Christians sometimes use? How do we locate religious experiences in "good feelings" rather than in the will? How do you think that false spirituality denies the Word made flesh? How does it disparage the world that God has created?

The Apostles' Creed reads: "I believe in the Holy Spirit, the holy catholic Church, the communion of saints, the forgiveness of sins, the resurrection of the body, and the life everlasting." Here is affirmed the work of the Holy Spirit in our lives, the universal church, the blessings of the Christian community, our forgiveness and a new start, the resurrection of the body, and the persistence of our individual personality into eternity. By the resurrection of the body we mean to affirm the unity of the person—body, mind, and spirit. The words symbolize the goodness of our material existence and the persistence by God's grace of the unique individual human being.

How have members of the class known the Word to reach them through their involvement with mundane and commonplace experience? How do they think the Holy Spirit meets us in the work place and the marketplace? Do you think the Holy Spirit brings joy to our work? How? If the task of the Holy Spirit is to help us remember all that Jesus did and taught us, is there any sphere of life that the Spirit does not touch? If it does touch the wholeness of our lives, what actions must it necessarily prompt?

John 21:15-23. The questioning of Peter dominates the conversation here. Peter has come to the time of restoration following his cowardly refusal to be identified as a disciple of his Lord. Christ wants now to begin preparing Peter for the role he will play as the leader of the church.

"Do you love me more than these?" This key question is asked three times. The risen Lord asks us the same question. What stands in the way of our full commitment to him? We are called to give it up, as the rich young ruler was called to give up his possessions to follow Jesus.

Christ would have us remove the barriers to his love, the barriers that prevent our being fully human. Are we half-hearted in our allegiance to Christ? He would unify divided persons so that we can act with a single mind. Augustine said that the secret of Christian education is to get the weight of the learner's love rightly directed. This is precisely what Christ does with Peter and with us. He deals with the question of our chief love first. What do we love most? Can we love the Christ more than these? If so, Christ can restore us to our rightful place in his Kingdom.

When have we, like Simon Peter, turned our backs on Christ? When have we refused to follow him? Let us note that we are first asked to love the Lord—then by our love of the neighbor (anyone in need) Christ can know that we love him. Think of the most disreputable characters you know. Can you love them? Can you love all people—the hungry children across the world? the street people of our own towns? the men and women humiliated by unemployment? the people who are ill in body and mind and spirit? people who are different in ways we feel are dangerous? those who claim with their words to believe in and act for God, but whose actions thoroughly betray the love of God?

When we consider the enormity of the problems of serving Christ's people today, many Christians are prone to despair. Human suffering is vast, and people of good will are often frustrated about what to do. There is no shortage of religious and philanthropic agencies soliciting our money and support.

What can we do? Ask group members to suggest creative and constructive ways of tending and feeding Christ's sheep. Not all of these needs involve money. These actions might point us in the direction of changing our attitudes. In Christian thinking the individual human being is of infinite, absolute value. Each bears the image of God, no matter how that image may have been defaced by sin. Can Christians be bitter and stingy toward the poor? the unfortunate and suffering? Do we need to rethink our giving? Do we know how our money for charities is managed? Do we require that agencies send us audited financial reports? What is our church doing to meet human need?

The needs are enormous in our home churches, in our local communities, in our nation, and throughout the world. Our efforts may seem feeble in view of the world's need. But the love of Christ supports us when we are inclined to underestimate ourselves and our efforts for those who are hungry, sick, homeless, and in prison. What we do may augment the services of innumerable others and prove that the victorious Christ is using us in making all things new. Christ requires only that we trust him and give ourselves for love of him so that no matter how hard the circumstances, we may serve the world he came to save.

Jesus said, "Follow me!" Finally, Simon Peter got the message.

An old story that Christians have remembered across the centuries tells that Peter escaped from prison on the night before he was to be crucified. Peter was fleeing along the Appian Way when he met Jesus carrying a cross. "Lord, whither goest thou?" asked Peter. And the reply came, "I am going to Rome to be crucified afresh." Peter returned to his cell. When the guards came for him the next day, Peter was there. Christ's love had made him captive.

Peter faced prison and martyrdom, but what of John?

We do not know if John the beloved disciple went to prison for his faith, if he was martyred, or if he lived until a natural end. But we do know that John's vocation was to bear witness to the truth of the gospel of Christ. Peter wants to know what John's role and fate will be, and he asks Jesus a speculative question: "Lord, what about him?" Jesus tells Peter that the future of John is no concern of Peter's. His duty is to follow Christ. John has his own vocation, his own way of expressing his talents and gifts. Peter is to be a witness for the truth, following Christ above everything else.

John 21:24-25. The story has been told. It is a reliable witness to a story with reaches more vast, the unending account of what Christ is doing in the world.

He is alive, working within the church and within the world and in each of us to bring about the Kingdom that endures forever.

DIMENSION THREE:
WHAT DOES THE BIBLE MEAN TO ME?

The Christian Life Is a Victorious Life

In a scholarly book entitled *God Was in Christ: An Essay on Incarnation and Atonement*, British theologian D. M. Baillie has summed up what the New Testament says about human sin and Christ's victory over it. He sees the essence of sin as self-centeredness that destroys the individual and human community. Baillie, in the male-centric language of his day, gives a brief picture of our human life as it ought to be:

> I would tell a tale of God calling His human children to form a great circle for the playing of His game. In that circle we ought all to be standing, linked together with lovingly joined hands, facing towards the Light in the centre, which is God ("the Love that moves the sun and the other stars"); seeing our fellow creatures all round the circle in the light of that central Love, which shines on them and beautifies their faces; and joining with them in the dance of God's great game, the rhythm of love universal. But instead of that, we have, each one, turned our backs upon God and the circle of our fellows, and faced the other way, so that we can see neither the Light at the centre nor the faces on the circumference. And indeed in that position it is difficult even to join hands with our fellows! Therefore instead of playing God's game we play, each one, our own selfish little game, like the perverse children Jesus saw in the market-place, who would not join in the dance with their companions. Each one of us wishes to be the centre, and there is blind confusion, and not even any true knowledge of God or of our neighbours. That is what is wrong with mankind. Of course a man is not really happy in that attitude and situation, since he was created for community with God and man.[3]

Baillie goes on to show how the resurrected Christ draws us out of ourselves into the life of unselfish community.

God has never given up on us. He has sent Jesus to live out amid a sinful humanity the life of love. Jesus taught, labored, suffered, and died at last on a cross, forsaken and alone. But God brought him through death, raising him up and giving him back to us in an unseen way, the Holy Spirit that made Jesus' followers into a community.

Now, looking back, we can know that all this was in fact the love of God dealing with our sin, offering us forgiveness and a new start. So God's love in Christ creates a new person, a new community everywhere it is accepted.

We come confessing: "Not I, but the grace of God." That reality of God's redemption shatters the barriers between persons and between nations; for it is "the new People of God, the new Israel, the Ecclesia, the Body of Christ, the Church."[4] In these the risen Christ says to us anew, "Take heart! I have overcome the world."

---

[1] From *The Gospel of John*, Volume 2, revised edition, by William Barclay (Westminster, 1975), page 284.

[2] From *The Aims of Education*, by Alfred North Whitehead (Free Press, 1967).

[3] From *God Was in Christ: An Essay on Incarnation and Atonement*, by D. M. Baillie (Charles Scribner's Sons, 1948), page 206.

[4] From *God Was in Christ*, page 208.

CPSIA information can be obtained
at www.ICGtesting.com
Printed in the USA
LVHW01s1515171117
556605LV00004B/4/P

9 781501 848599